anarchist pocketbooks

SABATE
Guerrilla Extraordinary

Antonio Tellez

Introduction by Alfredo M. Bonanno

Elephant Editions
AK Press

Original title:
La Guerriglia Urbana in Spagna: Sabate

Translated by Stuart Christie

Cover illustration and design by
Clifford Harper

First English edition published in 1974 by
Davis-Poynter Limited
Book club edition published in 1974 by
Cienfuegos Press

First pocketbook edition published in 1985 by Elephant
Editions in co-edition with Refract Publications

This re-print published in Catania, August 1998,
by Elephant Editions in co-edition with AK Press

CONTENTS

CONTENTS

PREFACE

With this, the first in our edition of anarchist pocketbooks, we are opening the way to a series of instruments for use by anarchist comrades and all those who have decided to make their desire for freedom become reality. The series will be as many-faceted as anarchism itself, offering a critique of the great institutions of oppression: religion, economics, authority, ideology, even in their most subtle forms; a look at the field of art and aesthetics; at moments in the past where freedom was fought for and won, trying to see where things went wrong and what we can still apply today; proposals of new methods of struggle to be discussed and experimented.

We are doing this as a contribution to the struggle that is always in course, not as something separate to be set aside and chewed upon while we wait for better times. The value of this contribution to the great task of the revolution depends therefore not only upon our own efforts and constance, but also on the comrades we reach: that you do not treat these pages as a commodity, but enter into a living dialogue where words and deeds confuse themselves in the great turmoil of destruction and creation that knows no bounds and which with reason and passion we call anarchy.

The present volume is therefore not a history book full of mummies to be taken out, dusted, then returned to the order of the past. On the contrary, a dynamic reading of the experiences of Sabate and others could be a force in the moving of the somewhat still waters of the present.

Elephant Editions

INTRODUCTION

This book tells of the life, the action and the death of an anarchist guerilla.

Many things have happened since it was first published at the end of the sixties, and experience of armed struggle in Europe is no longer limited to that of the comrades who carried on the struggle against Francoist Spain. But that does not in the least detract from the theoretical and practical importance of Sabate's actions, and the value of this book in particular.

The discourse could be a long one, but let us try to shorten it so as not to complicate things.

It would seem that all anarchists should agree on certain points; not hold exactly the same opinion, but at least be without any major contradictions. The first such issue is that of *attacking the class enemy* (i.e. the exploiter), both in the macroscopic aspect of the State and in the microscopic one of the individual responsible for exploitation. Yet when a comrade organises to pass from words to deeds, those who come forward with doubts, perplexity, suspicions, uncertainty, are never lacking. There are always some anarchist comrades who have turned their anarchism into a kind of windshield to hide their own weakness and compromise. They obviously cannot approve of anyone who contributes to unmasking them with their actions, of who, by attacking the enemy rouses the still waters of sleep, often attracting the attention of the forces of repression.

Such criticism as, "The time isn't right", "These things are only done when the revolution is near", "We must wait to be sure the masses are with us", are constantly aimed at the comrade who intends to act *now, right away.*

As far as Sabate's actions are concerned, he, in practice, was left alone with only a few comrades who from time to time united with him individually to continue the struggle. But these actions had to take place inside Spain. When it came to wanting to do something outside to strike the fascist regime, there was a flood of disagreement. And also, later, when there was recourse to international collaboration (for example the kidnapping of monsignor Ussia), there were not a few dissenters. The fact that the action was to be seen in the light of its exceptional objective of saving the lives of comrades who had been sentenced to death was also underlined.

The reader will realise that little or nothing has changed since the time when Sabate carried out his struggle in complete isolation. Even in very recent times, when anarchists have organised to *attack*, the so-called 'official' movement has preferred to remain silent, that is, when it has not come out with declarations of doubt or outright condemnation.

Is this the ineluctable destiny of all organisations? We do not believe so. An organisation that defines itself as custodian of the anarchist movement's ideological traditions must necessarily become conservative and regard all initiatives of attack—especially when not under its control—with preoccupation and suspicion. On the contrary, an organisation born as a structure of attack, capable of modifying itself according to the needs of the moment, that avoids bureaucratisation and has no intention of keeping any 'memory', can become the indispensable basis for revolutionary action. And, basically, it is towards this kind of organisation that Sabate's efforts went, as with any other anarchist revolutionary who intends to attack the class enemy.

It is precisely on either side of this separating line that two different models of intervention develop.

On the one hand, the counter-informative model as an end in itself, a structure eternally repeating itself, that survives in its own image, from time to time supplying more advanced opinions on what the forces of power decide to circulate.

On the other hand, a minimal structure organising in order to act, that keeps well documented on reality, but only in order to bring about projects of intervention and revolutionary actions, not to distribute it for consumerism. In this perspective everything takes on a different light. In the first place the availability of means. Whoever limits themselves to counter-information bases themselves on the good will of comrades and their subscriptions. Whoever has a precise project of attack must go further, expropriating the necessary finance from the capitalists. But then the level of engagement is also different, in the latter case complete and total.

Of course there are risks. Not so much of life, which for a revolutionary is always at stake in all his decisions, as of separation, isolation.

The imbecility of others, their bad faith in not wanting to understand, their tepidness: all these wound mortally, often more than the enemy's bullets. Interested sympathy is also harmful, as is morbid curiosity.

And Sabate was wounded by all these painful thorns in his side before being killed by the Guardia Civile.

But he never stopped, never drew back. He never let himself be overcome by doubt. And let it not be said (as it has been said) that things were easier for him because we all agree about combatting fascism. That is all right for the hypocrits who disguise themselves as revolutionaries, certainly not for anarchists. Fascism is always before us, even when it wears the multicoloured clothing of Mrs Thatcher's relatively permissive welfare State.

Everyone understands that quite easily. Less easily do they decide to act. That is why a book of this kind is always useful: because reading it pushes one to action, arouses enthusiasm. Because it shows the thousand and one ways in which it is possible to strike the enemy, because it gives no space to resignation and doubt.

It is necessary to understand that we cannot wait for others—not even for other comrades—to give us the sign to act, the final indication. This *must come from us*. Each one of us, taken individually, must find his or her own comrades and constitute *small affinity groups* which are the essential element for giving life to the organisa-

11

tion of attack that we need. Actions will come easily, as a natural consequence of the decision to act together against the common enemy. Grand words, declarations to go down in history, the great organisations of the glorious past and vast programmes for the future are all useless if the will of the individual comrade is lacking.

And in this perspective Sabate was never alone. His struggle is still continuing today.

Alfredo M. Bonanno

CHAPTER I

Sabate

Manuel Sabate belonged to the Guardia Urbana[1] in the little town of Hospitalet de Llobregat,[2] which, with its seventy thousand inhabitants, is part of the great sprawling complex of Barcelona. His wife, Madrona Llopart, self-denying, hard working, completely dedicated to the care of her house and family, was a typical Spanish housewife.

They had five children. Three of them play a part in our story: Jose, the eldest, born in 1910; Francisco, born on 30 March, 1915; Manuel, born in 1927. The fourth Juan, and a sister, Maria, never took part in the brothers' activities. Francisco, better known by the Catalan diminutive of his name Sisco, Sisquet or Quico, was self-confident and showed strength of character even as a boy.

The parents, completely ignorant of conditions in the reformatories of the day and badly advised, decided to send their indomitable boy to the Duran Home in Barcelona when he was only seven years old. This institution, controlled by friars, was really a penitentiary establishment for minors. The Duran Home became a nursery school for rebels. Another of its pupils was Mariano Rodriguez Vazquez, known by the diminutive of Marianet, who later became General Secretary[3] during the Spanish Civil War of the National Confederation of Labour, the CNT,[4] the most important of all trade unions in Spain.

During the Civil War the Duran Home was razed to the

13

ground and the community of friars dissolved. After the war they re-formed and bought the farm Torre Vilana, in one of the most aristocratic suburbs of Barcelona, complete with modern fixtures. The discipline, however, remained on the familiar lines of the old building.[5]

At the time *El Quico*[6] was there its prison discipline, with its many humiliations and corporal punishment, touched off a chord in him, and for ever after he fought for justice and liberty. It did not take long for him to reach the end of his tether, and one day the boy climbed the wall of the yard, using a tree and improvised rope, and returned home. On his knees he begged his parents not to send him back to the Institution, saying that if they did he would immediately escape again – this time for ever. He promised to be a 'good' boy if only they would not take him back and, between pleas and threats, it did not take long for him to get his own way.

Education in Spain at this time was of little concern to the Government. National schools were scarce, and the private fee-paying schools were in the hands of monks and Marists,[7] out of the reach of ordinary workers, more so those with large families like *El Quico*'s. School teachers in Spain were not held in great social esteem. There was no humour in the popular phrase 'to be as hungry as a school teacher' – it was not a profession one sought. For thousands of children, the only school was the street, and later, the workshop, where they went as apprentices at the age of ten or less. *El Quico* was no exception to the rule and his apprenticeship as a plumber was a normal one : the greater part of it consisting of cuffs and abuse, which he took badly.

At the first opportunity he joined the General Union of Hospitalet, affiliated to the CNT, and it was to this organization that he remained faithful for the rest of his life – in spirit if not in discipline. He joined just before the Proclamation of

14

the Republic in 1931. The 'workers' Republic was everything except what its name indicated. It inherited all the vices and corrupt institutions of the monarchy. It took over the Army, which was always ready to intervene in political life and which abhorred all democratic institutions. It made room for the absolute church, with its countless religious orders and their obscurantist mentality, sworn enemy of culture and progress. It tolerated feudalism on the land where landlords and aristocrats lorded it over the most frightful misery of half Spain. It maintained a sterile and corrupt bureaucracy.

The Proclamation of the Republic gave rise to riotous popular demonstrations of support. It was thought to be the advent of a new era; two days later, however, on 16 April, the Minister of the Interior, Miguel Maura, said to reporters: 'I should like you to make it understood in your newspapers that I am not prepared to allow for one more hour any further demonstrations in the streets. The people are getting out of hand! Everything is degenerating rapidly into an unacceptable public scandal!'

Maura's[8] arrogant behaviour on this occasion cannot be put down to a simple case of nerves: throughout his career he showed symptoms of being a chronic pathological case. This Catholic and Republican gentleman demonstrated to the world his true character when, a few weeks later – on 23 July, he ordered the Army to destroy the Anarcho-Syndicalist meeting place in Seville, a bar called Casa de Cornelio situated in La Macarena. Three artillery pieces fired twenty-two high explosive shells into the old bar, reducing it to ruins.

The new Republic took an immediate stand against the people who had for years demanded major changes in the economic and social life of Spain. It turned viciously against the very people who had brought it to life. The social agitation in Spain during the period of the Republic need not be described here in detail, but in order to give some idea of the revolutionary spirit of the people (later to become the first in Europe to rise against fascism) we may mention the insurrectionary movement of 18 January, 1932 in the mining area of Alto Llobregat y Cardoner in the Catalan Pyrenees. The Anarcho-Syndicalists in Figols and Sallent declared for libertarian communism, abolishing all private property and the circulation of money in their villages. However, within five days the revolutionary workers' movement had been destroyed after a bitter struggle. The last bulwark of the revolution, Cardoner, fell on 22 January. The repression which followed throughout Catalonia was bitter. In the dark dawn of 11 February the ship *Buenos Aires* sailed for Bata in Spanish Guinea[9] from Barcelona with 104 confederal militants aboard, among them Buenaventura Durruti Dumanger[10] and Francisco Ascaso Abadia.[11] Meanwhile, throughout the northern provinces the Army and the Police applied the *ley de fuga*,[12] filling the cemeteries and prisons with their working-class victims.

Popular protests against the deportations and police violence were expressed by many strikes throughout Spain, and sometimes even by new insurrections, such as that which took place at Tarrasa on 14 February, where the people took to the streets and for some hours were in full control of the situation; taking over the Town Hall, arresting the Mayor and all the reactionary functionaries they came across. The red and black flag of the CNT-FAI flew proudly over the Town Hall. Troops were quickly sent from Barcelona, however, and soon managed to regain control of the town. Forty-two men were arrested and charged under military law. When they were brought to trial the prosecutor demanded forty-two sentences of death.[13]

The peasants of Hospitalet also went on strike at this time in protest against the feudal conditions under which they were being forced to work. The landlords would not give way and the strike dragged on. With no money coming in the labourers and their families were literally starving. *El Quico* and another young Anarchist comrade decided to help in the defence of the peasants – in their own way. They robbed one of the most important of the local landlords, taking every peseta he had in his possession. The money collected was given to the strike committee to be distributed to the families most in need.

Reaction soon hit back. The news that General Jose Sanjurjo y Sacanell, Head of the Carabineros, and the ex-head of the Guardia Civil[14] was preparing a military uprising was common knowledge. The Sanjurjo conspiracy[15] exploded on 10 August, 1932 in Madrid and Seville, but two months previously, on 9 June, in a question to the Cortes about the situation in Seville,[16] Deputy Miguel Garcia Bravo Ferrer read out a leaflet which had been circulating in the Andalusian capital and was signed by the Committee of Revolutionary Workers and Soldiers:

> The Guardia Civil under the criminal Sanjurjo is preparing to establish in Spain a murderous dictatorship. Citizens, prepare yourselves for the hour of struggle has arrived. Soldiers, citizens and workers – together we shall fight against Sanjurjo and the Guardia Civil.[17] Grasp the gun which you have in your hand and fulfil your obligations. People: *Viva la anarquia!*

In Madrid, however, the rising was successful only in gaining control of the Ministries of War and Communication.

Castilblanco was a village of four thousand inhabitants in the province of Badajoz. On 1 January, 1932 five hundred striking peasants held a demonstration there which was broken up by the Guardia Civil with volleys of rifle-fire. Enraged, the villagers attacked the defenders of the absentee landlords and at the end of the day the tally was four guards and one peasant

17

killed, with a number of demonstrators badly wounded. The villagers charged with the deaths of the Guardia Civil were sentenced to death, but public protest was so great that the authorities were forced to commute their sentences, and they were eventually granted an amnesty.[18]

In Arnedo (Logroño) on 5 January the Guardia Civil once again attacked a demonstration with rifle-fire. Women and children were present on the demonstration, and the result was a veritable slaughter. Six people died – amongst them four women – and thirty-two people were wounded. The indignation throughout Spain was unanimous, and this was the prime cause of Sanjurjo's dismissal. The man who took his place, General Miguel Cabanellas, was another equally perfidious figure in the history of Spain.

In Seville, the Anarcho-Syndicalists declared a General Strike, and stormed the barracks. Thus, ironically, they saved the Republic which had so cruelly persecuted them. It was in this period of permanent social unrest that Sabate formed, along with other young men, one of the first action groups – 'Los Novatos'. The eldest of the group was Jose, El Quico's brother, who was then twenty-two years of age. Los Novatos was affiliated to the local Federation of the Iberian Anarchist Federation.[19] The group went into major action almost immediately. On 8 January, 1933, there erupted a new revolutionary movement inspired by the FAI to protest against the systematic and tenacious political persecution of the workers by the Government, led by Manuel Azaña y Diaz, an adept and capable persecutor. In Zaragoza and Barcelona numerous arrests were made before there was any hint of revolution. However, the protest movement erupted in many places. In Ribarroja and other villages of the Levante, libertarian communism was declared and other attempts followed in Andalusia.

In Casas Viejas, in the Cadiz area, the Republic acted with

a savagery rarely equalled in its history. A seventy-year-old peasant, Francisco Cruz, better known as '*Seisdedos*' ('six fingers'), refused to surrender to the Assault Guards. Together with his family and like-minded libertarians who desired social justice, he barricaded himself in a farmhouse. The Republican mercenaries bombarded the building and killed them all, women and children as well, in accordance with the orders of Prime Minister Azaña:[20]

'Do not spare the wounded, do not take prisoners. Shoot them down like dogs.'[21]

As a result of this order by the future President, of the twenty-four who fought, twenty-four were left dead.

In the summer of 1933, Sabate's group attended one of the many meetings organized by the FAI. It was a place well-known to them, Fuente del Oso, on a mountain near Esplugas, in the district of San Feliu de Llobregat, and it was there that they met to practise arms-drill and the handling of explosives. While the meeting was in full swing the sentries at the access to the site warned of the approach of two truck-loads of Guardia Civil and Mozos de Escuadra – the Catalan militia, organized by the Generalitat from among gamekeepers, to put down poachers and trespassers. The meeting broke up. Some escaped easily through the nearby pine wood, while others, to divide their forces, ran quickly through open country. Among the latter was *El Quico*. The chase went on for over half an hour with constant shooting, but happily the *faistas* suffered no losses or wounds. It was the baptism of fire for *Los Novatos*. Next day, the CNT central trade union daily *Solidaridad Obrera* published a front-page article under the title 'Empty bag at the pine-wood'.

At about this time the elections were announced for 19 November, 1933. The CNT urged total abstention in the voting. During the pre-electoral period the Confederation poured out an immense amount of propaganda and in the final period organized a mass meeting in the monumental Plaza de Toros in Barcelona, in which well-known militants of the CNT/FAI, such as Buenaventura Durruti, participated. The slogan of the anti-election campaign was 'power to the people – not politicians'. The right wing won the election, and the CNT carried out its promise. On 8 December, 1933 insurrection broke out again in Barcelona, Zaragoza, Valencia, and Granada, however, the heat of the revolution was in the Aragon and Rioja regions where once again the red and black flag flew above the villages which had declared for libertarian communism. *Los Novatos*, who had made intense preparations to participate in the revolution, launched themselves into the streets, where they easily overcame the government forces in Hospitalet, taking control of every official centre in the town, and collecting all the records and files they could lay their hands on (these latter provided exceptionally good fuel for the many bonfires organized during the festivities which followed). The insurrection was eventually put-down on the 14th, but only after many dead and wounded had thinned the ranks of the workers. Thousands of *cenetistas* went to prison. In Zaragoza, the whole of the National Committee of the CNT was arrested, as was the Revolutionary Committee, which included Buenaventura Durruti, Cipriano Mera Sanz and Isaac Puente Amestoy.[22] *Solidaridad Obrera* was banned, although it had suffered its first governmental suspension in 1933. Between then and 1934 (the day before the insurrection of the Generalitat) it was suspended three times, once for 104 days. Single editions were impounded thirty-four times.[23]

The Sabate brothers managed to escape the repression, but the prisons of Spain were filled with anarcho-syndicalist militants.

Nevertheless, the repression did not prevent the calling of

many more bitter strikes, and an unequalled rise in the feeling of resistance. The most outstanding was the General Strike in Zaragoza. May Day was celebrated in the Aragon capital with a complete and total withdrawal of labour. The employers sacked all their workers. The Trade Unions then declared a General Strike to demand the reinstatement of the dismissed men, and, as neither side would give in, the city remained paralysed for thirty-six days. The strikers were reduced to complete misery. The editor of *Solidaridad Obrera*, Manuel Villar Mingo,[24] organized a subscription to send the children of the strikers to Catalonia to alleviate their distress and help their parents win the battle. The subscription had an unprecedented success and within a few days the offices of '*Soli*' had accumulated what was, for that period, a considerable sum of money. The people of Barcelona prepared to receive the first influx of children from Zaragoza, due to arrive at the headquarters of the confederal newspaper at six o'clock on a Sunday evening. A large number of people gathered outside the print shop to await their arrival. To prevent this act of solidarity the Generalitat stepped in. Without any previous warning they stopped the buses bringing the children and opened fire on the demonstrators – many of them women and children – killing one workman and wounding others. As a result of the public outcry *Solidaridad Obrera* was banned by government decree yet again. The buses were diverted and did not arrive in Barcelona until after a long delay. The children were then handed over to the workers' families who had been waiting to receive them.[25]

In reply to this act of provocation, the Catalan Regional Committee of the CNT decided as a protest to call a twenty-four-hour General Strike in the capital of the principality. The decision announcing the General Strike was to be made in a public manifesto. Francisco Sabate and another youth were given the job of collecting the documents. They were to meet in the bar 'La Tranquilidad' in the centre of Barcelona, the Paralelo. When the two friends arrived at the prearranged spot, comrades there told them that the manifesto had to be collected from a bar in Montjuich. While they were waiting at this bar the police arrived, arresting everyone present. *El Quico* experienced for the first time a taste of prison. He spent a night in the cells of the commissariat of Pueblo Seco, and a day in the Palacio de Justicia where his case was heard, followed by two days in the Model Prison of Barcelona. The charge 'clandestine meetings' would not stick, and after seventy-two hours everyone was released.

On 6 October, 1934 insurrection broke out again and for fifteen victorious days all the forces of the Left in the Asturias joined under the common slogan, 'unite, proletarian brothers!' (UHP), but in Catalonia the rising was a disaster, as it was Nationalist in inspiration and the CNT-FAI made no attempt to intervene. The *Los Novatos* group dedicated itself to collecting the arms which had been dumped in the streets and sewers by the men of the Generalitat. It was these arms which later helped crush the fascist uprising in Catalonia in July 1936. *El Quico* received his conscription papers in 1935, but as a convinced anti-militarist he did not present himself, and was posted as a deserter. It was also about this time he carried out his first act of expropriation to help the funds of the Political Prisoners' Aid Committee at the expense of the Bank of Gava, a village of 6,000 inhabitants in the county of San Feliu de Llobregat, just outside Barcelona. Towards the end of 1935 he met Leonor Castells Marti, the woman who was to be his companion throughout the years to come. Soon after he met her, after a bare six months of peaceful life, Spain exploded. It was 18 July, 1936.

Leonor says in one of her letters:

22

I remember it as though it were yesterday. After many days of meetings, without sleeping and almost without any meals the comrades came to the little house we had built with love and hard work. Francisco, always active and courageous went from my side, one could almost say forever . . . The revolution had started – Francisco hugged me and I held him in my arms for a few moments and then he was gone.

[1] The Municipal Guard, Guardia Urbana, was controlled by the local councils and under the orders of the Mayor. It controlled traffic and enforced the regulations of the Urban Police.

[2] The population of Hospitalet has grown considerably since the beginning of the century. Since 1962 its population has risen from 150,000 to 250,000 in 1972.

[3] Mariano R. Vazquez was born in Barcelona in 1909. He was drowned while bathing near Paris in the River Marne on 18 June, 1939. See the book *Manuel Munoz Diez: Marianet, Semblanza de un Hombre,* Ed. CNT, Mexico, 1960.

[4] The Confederacion Nacional de Trabajo was formed during the National Congress of Labour held in the Palacio de Bellas Artes in Barcelona on 30 October-1 November 1910. It was influenced by the Bakunist ideas of the First International.

[5] This 'educational establishment' is fully described in Michel de Castillo's book *Tanguy,* Ed. Julliard, Paris 1957 – the Home is referred to as the 'Asile Dumos, Centre de Redressement'.

[6] After Sabate's death a number of journalists interpreted this name as a derivative of Chico, Pequeno, meaning small or little. This was not the case as Sabate was of robust constitution, agile and quite tall (5 foot 9 inches).

[7] A religious order whose name derives from the 'Followers of Mary', founded in Lyons in the XIX Century by Abbot Colin for the purpose of 'educating young people'.

[8] Miguel Maura was born in Madrid in 1887. He was succeeded as Minister of the Interior, on 14 October, 1931, by Santiago Cesares Quiroga – a politician as unpopular as his predecessor. Maura died in Zaragoza in 1971.

[9] Fernando Poo and Rio Muñi, in Spanish Equatorial Guinea, obtained their independence in 1968; the territory of Ifni was finally returned to

23

Morocco by the Treaty of Fez signed on 4 January, 1969.

[10] Durruti, one of the most outstanding figures of Spanish Anarchism, was born in Leon on 14 July, 1896. He died on the Madrid front in the area of University City on 20 November, 1936. (See *Durruti, The People in Arms* by Abel Paz, Ed. de la Tête de Feuilles, Paris 1972.)

[11] Ascaso, born 1 April, 1909 in Almudebar. Inseparable comrade of Durruti, he died in Barcelona on 20 July, 1936 during the assault on the Atarazanas Barracks which had risen in support of Franco. His elder brother, Domingo, was killed during the events of May 1937 in Barcelona.

[12] The *ley de fuga* – a law which permitted the shooting of those who tried to escape from the clutches of the forces of law and order. It was the brain-child of General Severiano Martinez Anido, Governor of Barcelona, and was applied from 1920 onwards. It was the easiest legal method of eliminating the oustanding spokesmen and militants of the workers' organizations; the authorities would release the prisoners from police stations and prisons and, as they made their way homewards, they were massacred in the street, shot in the back by machine-gun fire. In the files it was recorded simply as 'an attempted escape'.

[13] See *Solidaridad Obrera* of Barcelona, 7 April, 1933. The sentences actually received were four of twenty years and one day, six of six years and a day, two acquitted and four dismissed. The others received sentences of twelve years and one day, according to Diego Abad de Santillan in his book *Contribution to the History of the Working Class Movement in Spain*, Volume 3, Ed. Cajica, Mexico 1971.

[14] Sanjurjo was dismissed as Director-General of the Guardia Civil on 8 January, 1932, as a result of the incidents in Castilblanco and Arnedo. The President, Manuel Azana, as compensation, offered him the Director-Generalship of the Carabineros.

[15] Sanjurjo, Marquis of Rif, was the moving spirit behind the 'National Rising' in 1936. Born in Pamplona on 28 March, 1872, he died on 21 July, 1936 in Portugal when the aeroplane carrying him to Spain crashed. On his death the leadership passed to General Francisco Franco.

[16] Bravo Ferrer, the Radical deputy for Seville, made a dramatic statement about the situation in the Andalusian capital, which can be concisely summed-up as follows: during the three-month period from October to December 1931 there were three hundred partial strikes in Seville and a large number of bombs exploded. There was a rapid increase in the number of robberies and '*attentats*'. The victims were numbered in dozens.

[17] The Guardia Civil, in contradiction to its name, is a uniformed military corps, controlled directly from the Ministry of the Army and the Spanish Ministry of the Interior. In 1940 it was merged with the Carabineros. Formed by the second Duke of Ahumada in 1844 to combat banditry, it was very soon entrusted with governmental, judicial, fiscal and police work. In 1969 the Guardia Civil numbered 60,000 men.

[18] Quoted by Jaoquin Arraras in his *History of the Second Spanish Republic*, Editora Nacional, Madrid 1969.

[19] The FAI (Federacion Anarquista Iberica) was formed during the dictatorship of General Miguel Primo de Rivera, at the National Anarchist Conference held in Valencia on 25/26 July, 1927.

[20] Azaña was born in Alcalà de Henares in 1880. He died on 1 November, 1940 in Montauban (France), shortly after stepping down from the Presidency of the Republic.

[21] In fact, one did manage to escape from Casa Viejas, although badly wounded – Maria Silva Cruz, called 'La Libertaria', the grand-daughter of Francisco Cruz and the daughter of Juan Silva, another of the victims. She survived until August 1936, when she was murdered by Francoist troops on the Jerez road, in Medina Sidonia.

[22] Cipriano Mera, born November 1897, fled to North Africa after the Civil War but was handed over in 1942 by the Pétain Government to the Spanish Authorities who had demanded his extradition. He was condemned to death the following year, but his sentence was later commuted to life imprisonment. He was paroled in 1946 and went to France where, he worked as a bricklayer, retiring recently at the age of seventy-four.

Isaac Puente, a doctor from Alava and a leading anarchist theoretician, was murdered by Franco forces in July 1936.

[23] For further information see Manuel Villar, *El Anarquismo en la Insurreccion de Asturias*, Ed. Nervio, Buenos Aires 1936.

[24] Apart from being the editor of '*Soli*' and the Valencia paper *Fragua Social* he had also run *La Protesta* in Buenos Aires until his expulsion from the Argentine. Arrested at the end of the Civil War, he was freed a few months later, only to be imprisoned once again in 1941 for his activities against the Franco régime. He was not released until April 1946.

In May 1947 Enrique Marcos Nadal, Secretary of the clandestine National Committee of the CNT, was arrested in Barcelona, and his place was taken by Villar. On 20 November Villar was arrested in Madrid and in January 1949 he was brought before a Council of War in Ocaña and sentenced to twenty-five years imprisonment. He died in Buenos Aires in 1972.

[25] Other transfers of children were organized, one of them by miners of Sallent. Another destined for Barcelona, was intercepted by Assault Guards and the children taken to a hospice, from which the parents of the children were ordered to collect them. Eventually, as a result of these acts of solidarity, the workers of Zaragoza won their struggle.

CHAPTER II

The Civil War

On 18 July, 1936, the fascist uprising broke out and the militants of the CNT-FAI immediately made their preparations for the confrontation. Francisco and Jose joined the local Defence Group and Revolutionary Committee of Hospitalet, which had anticipated the rising, and on their own initiative raided the houses of known fascists and sympathisers a few days before the *pronunciamento*. That way they managed to collect arms and also cut off the possible roots of support for the uprising in the area. In a day they had the situation in Hospitalet well in hand, and were free to help their comrades in Barcelona on the 19th. The military rebellion was put down in Catalonia within a few days and the majority of Sabate's group, *Los Novatos*, left for the Aragon front on the 24th with a column led by Buenaventura Durruti, whose military adviser and second in command was Enrique Perez Farras.

On 27 August Jose and Francisco also left for the Aragon Front with *Los Aguiluchos*, the first column organized by the CNT-FAI in conjunction with the Militia Committee.[1] This column was organized by Juan Garcia Oliver and later, after the formation of the People's Army, it helped to make up two Confederal divisions under Miguel Garcia Vivancos[2] and Gregorio Jover Cortes.[3] Jose Sabate was made a centurion (responsible for one hundred men), while *El Quico* was made responsible for twenty men. The brothers' activities were neither more nor less outstanding than those of the thousands of others prepared to sacrifice their lives at the front rather than live under fascism. *El Quico*, anticipating the Cuban *barbudos* on the Sierra Maestra, grew his hair and beard long, saying he would not cut it until the peoples' triumph was complete throughout the peninsula. He did not get home leave in Barcelona until December. There, when he did arrive finally, he caused a minor sensation in the Plaza de España when he parked his car. The Russians had come! Everyone assumed him to be a *sovietico* – he never laughed more than he did that time when Militia men of all nationalities approached him trying out their recently-acquired Russian phrases.

Here we can mention how it came about that Francisco could be labelled by the Francoist Press, after his death, as a car thief. At that time the forces at the front, especially the confederal forces (those of the CNT-FAI) were always short of transport. It was the custom to pick out groups to go back to town to 'requisition' some of the huge quantity of vehicles used by the bureaucracy, and take them back to the front, where they were incorporated into the units. Sabate was then attached to the 126th Brigade, 28th Division (Ascaso), and it was his job to carry out this mission. One day, together with some of his friends in the 4th Battalion then at the Huesca Front (Almunia), Sabate 'requisitioned' a beautiful De Soto parked outside the Air Ministry and returned with it to the Brigade H.Q., where he was met with laughter and cheers by his comrades in arms. His friends pointed out that obviously such a magnificent machine would be spotted the moment it went into service, but *El Quico* had his own ideas on the subject and went ahead, ignoring the jokes. He stripped the rear of the car with an oxy-acetylene torch and welded to it the body of a disused service truck. A few coats of paint later and the beautiful De Soto was transformed into a serviceable van.

Soon afterwards Sabate was transferred to the 25th Division (ex-Ortiz Column) and, in his rank of armourer, took 'his' van with him.

In the middle of 1937 the Communist Party began its drive to seize control of the Army commands throughout Spain. The watchword of Moscow was 'who controls the army dictates the political orientation of the country'. The attempt was resisted strongly by the overwhelming majority of Spaniards, but unfortunately for the Spanish working class, the Party had its way, having used every possible means to put this dictum into effect.

At that time many young men were leaving for the Soviet Union to train as pilots. *El Quico* too, wanted to become a pilot, as he realized that the Air Force would prove to be the most decisive military arm of the war.

The Air Force, however, was totally controlled by the Communist Party[4] and to become a pilot it was necessary to be a member of the JSU (United Young Socialists),[5] or at the very least have a special recommendation as a *persona grata*. *El Quico* thought at one time of joining the JSU, if there was no other way; after all, as he said, 'the habit does not make the monk'. However, he was unable to put this idea into practice owing to a cataclysmic series of events which, as we shall see shortly, were to force him into anonymity for the rest of the war.

The 'Nationalist' campaign in the north ended with the conquest of Bilbao, Santander and Gijon. At that time the front stretched for over 1,800 kilometres – from the Pyrenees in the north, just east of Canfranc -- right down to Motril on the outskirts of Granada on the Mediterranean coast. Along this front there were a number of important individual Nationalist strongholds, such as that in the area of Teruel.

On 15 December Republican forces attacked the capital of Lower Aragon, Teruel. The Chief of Staff for the central area,

Lt-Colonel Vicente Rojo, prepared a force of approximately 100,000 men together with the necessary artillery, transport and aerial support for the offensive. Teruel finally surrendered to the Republican troops on 7 January, thus ending the offensive phase of the battle.

The Francoist counter-offensive developed rapidly and Sabate, who was one of the Republican troops sent to reinforce the sector being held by the 116th, 117th and 118th Mixed Brigades of the XXth Army Group, originally destined as one of the reserve units based in the small village of Corbalan, near Teruel, was redirected into the front line in order to contain the sudden advance of the National Armies.

One of the many methods used by the Communist Party in its struggle for complete control of the Army was to try literally to annihilate the Confederal forces. The tactic employed was usually that of sending Anarcho-Syndicalist units into the most dangerous positions, almost always headlong 'kamikaze' attacks which were certain to result in the slaughter of the libertarian troops. The major advantage of these mass murders, from the point of view of the Communist Party in its power struggle against the numerically stronger Anarcho-Syndicalist trade unions, was its legality. During one of these 'liquidation' operations, a Confederal company led by Communist officers lost eighty per cent of its combat force. The men were so furious that the General Staff were forced to recall the Captain and the Company Commissar, a man by the name of Ariño, to demand an explanation.

However, Sabate and three of his comrades were not content with official reprimands, and wanted to settle accounts properly. They prepared to waylay them – the 'mandarins', as Communist officials were derogatorily named by the troops – on their return from company headquarters. Commissar Ariño was first to return and, when he found his way blocked, he took out his gun prepared to force his way through. *El Quico*, always loath to shoot first, reacted quickly and shot him with one bullet, leaving him dying in the snow.

On their return to the battalion, the four friends realized that they might have been seen and seriously risked facing a firing squad, and so, Teruel already having been retaken by the Nationalists on 22 February, they decided to desert and set out for Barcelona. The war was as good as lost – the Republican defeat at Teruel, together with the enormous losses at the Battle of the Ebro some months later, had decided its course.

The four made their way to Barcelona, taking with them the De Soto. Two of Sabate's comrades were from Almudebar in the province of Huesca, one by the name of Matias and the other Alejandro – the third one's name is unknown to us. In Barcelona *El Quico* presented himself to the Regional Committee of the CNT and informed them of the incident with Commissar Ariño and requested that he be sent to a different Confederal unit where he could remain in safety. This was accepted but could not be done immediately, and he had to wait for some time in the Catalan capital. While he was in Barcelona the Defence Committee of the Young Libertarians asked him to undertake some risky missions – one of which was to liberate a comrade belonging to the Control Patrols,[6] who had been wounded and later arrested in a gun-fight with the forces of the Generalitat. The 'Checa'[7] was waiting for him to recover sufficiently before submitting him to their 'interrogation'. Sabate, together with Jaime Pares Adan – known as *El Abisinio* because of his Afro-type hair – carried out the rescue operation with complete success.

Another task which Sabate carried out successfully was organizing the escape of four comrades arrested following the 'events of May, 1937',[8] while they were being transferred from

Barcelona's Model Prison to the Castle of Montjuich.

Another action of Sabate at this time was an *attentat* against the locally-hated fascist, Justo Oliveras of Hospitalet. When the fascists rose, Oliveras, a man without scruples, managed to save his life by various devious stratagems and by going into hiding at the most crucial moment. In Hospitalet, it should be pointed out in passing, very few people were shot. Oliveras remained in hiding for a long period during which his haulage business was expropriated by the people. Later, when all the young people of the village and surrounding area were at the front, and the others setting to work trying to build a free society, Oliveras sensed that the moment of danger had passed and returned once again to circulation. He set out to regain and double all that the revolution had taken from him. He did this quite openly and brazenly, exploiting the people by supplying the necessities of life at exorbitant prices, and which only he could say how he had acquired.

Oliveras paid no attention to the constant warnings he received advising him to stop this bare-faced robbery of the people and, eventually, unable to stop him by any other means, *El Quico* paid him a visit. Sabate called at Oliveras' premises as he was closing his shop for the evening. Locking the door from the inside, Sabate left a comrade outside to stand guard, having made up his mind that Oliveras would never again return to exploit the people. The death of the black marketeer was never attributed to Sabate.

Another action in which Francisco took part had tragic consequences for one of the *Los Novatos* group, Francisco Aleu – better known as *El Nano de Sans*. One day Sabate met a friend of his from Hospitalet, a father with a large family, who had just received his conscription papers. He was full of despair at the idea of abandoning his children. Sabate, always anti-militarist and bitter about the revolutionary setbacks of the

31

war and the course it had taken, and indignant at the temporising attitude taken by the Spanish Anarchist Movement before the ever-encroaching Communist hegemony imposed by Moscow, decided to help him avoid the call-up. He told him he would supply him with forged documents which would allow him to remain in the rear with his family. A friend of *El Quico* who ran a small print shop undertook to print the false documents. Unfortunately, however, the police, suspecting the man, raided his workshop and caught him in the act of printing the forgeries. The printer was forced to confess the names of his customers and was obliged by the police to make a rendezvous with these people on some pretext. Suspecting nothing, two comrades – *El Nano de Sans* and Fontanet,[9] both members of *Los Novatos*, attended the rendezvous to see what the trouble was. *El Nano* was shot down the moment he set his foot in the door by a burst of machine-gun fire, but Fontanet managed to escape with only a bullet in his leg. Unfortunately for Sabate the police found his photograph in the pockets of the dead *El Nano*, as well as a list of addresses frequented by him. The police set out to arrest Sabate and finally ran him to ground coming out of a cinema one evening. Although armed, he found himself surrounded by police and could put up no real defence. This time he found himself in the hands of the SIM (Servicio Informacion Militar),[10] who had searched for him relentlessly in order to settle accounts for the death of Commissar Ariño.

Sabate realized that this was no laughing matter as, only a few days previously, Alejandro, one of the friends who had deserted with him, had been identified in Barcelona and shot down without warning or hesitation. Arriving at the police station – the Sans Commissariat – the SIM agents, who knew all about Sabate, decided to play a little game with him. In the interrogation room they had left one of their sub-machine guns on top of a table. They removed his handcuffs and made as if to leave the room but, as they had foreseen, *El Quico* fell for the bait and grabbed the weapon. As he did so, they rolled about on the floor with laughter. Foolishly, he realized that the gun was not loaded. They then proceeded to give him one of the worst beatings of his life.

When the Regional Committee of the CNT heard of Sabate's arrest they used all their influence to get him transferred to the Model Prison in Barcelona. They knew that in the cells of the 'Checa' he would be murdered without trial.[11] However, as the result of Sabate's arrest and the finding of some personal letters in his possession, the whereabouts of Matias, the third of the deserters came to light. Matias was in hospital in Aguas de Ribas, in Gerona, as the result of a wound received at the front. Luckily, in the next bed to him there was another comrade in the same battalion, Alejandro T., who, on seeing the 'Checa' arrive to arrest Matias, immediately telephoned the Secretary of the Catalan Regional Committee of the Libertarian Youth Movement, Ramon Liarte Siu. The immediate reaction from this quarter forced the 'Checa' to return Matias to hospital. Matias, knowing of Sabate's arrest and the death of Alejandro, did not believe the doctor would release him and managed to escape from his guarded hospital bed, taking refuge in the Confederal Remiro Battalion, where he remained until the end of the war, then escaping to France.[12]

Once in prison, Sabate's sole idea was to escape. There was a convenient cellar under his cell and whenever the opportunity presented itself he crawled through in an attempt to excavate a tunnel. This went on for weeks – slowly and patiently digging through the walls and foundations on his way to freedom. Just as he was on the point of completing his escape route the prison authorities barred up the entrance to the cellar, placing it out

of his reach. Resignation was a sentiment beyond the understanding of *El Quico* – 'so much work for nothing? – never!'

As the cellar was directly below his cell he set himself the
task of opening up a direct access to it. He succeeded and
could now continue his clandestine digging. He waded through
sewers – almost drowning in one of them – and broke his way
through solid walls. At long last he thought his efforts had been
rewarded. According to his calculations the only thing which
stood between him and freedom was one wall, but when he
finally broke through he found himself in an abandoned
cistern – still inside the prison. Without wasting any time he
searched for another exit, and hacking open a manhole cover,
was confronted by a ray of light shining in his face. He intended
to wait until night to effect his escape but that same day a
patrol discovered his patient labour and *El Quico* was taken
before the prison governor.

'They warned me to be careful of you but I did not pay
enough attention to them,' said the governor. 'What you have
done is absolutely frightening and if I had not seen it with my
own eyes I would have never believed it possible. You must
surely see it is my job to make sure you don't try again.'

Sabate was transferred to the punishment prison of Vic. His
failure in Barcelona did not make his chance of escape any
easier, so he decided to change his tactics. *El Quico* was receiving plenty of assistance from the outside in the way of money
and food. He thought that the most practical idea was to gain
the confidence and friendship of his warders through their
greed. He began to give large tips to the warders for the
slightest service. One day he bribed them to allow him to embrace his wife. From then on her visits became more and more
frequent until the warders got used to seeing her and did not
bother to search her in the usual way. Finally a prison officer
suggested that for a small consideration he could allow Sabate

to spend a few hours with his wife in an unoccupied cell. They agreed upon it, and the prison officer put a little bed in the cell as well. From then on he met his wife completely alone.

Seeing what an atmosphere of confidence he was building up, he suggested to Leonor that on her next visit she should bring with her a pistol and a hand-grenade. No sooner said than done. With the weapons in his possession he immediately began preparing an escape plan with three other comrades who were to go with him.

On the day planned for the escape, Sabate called the orderly, a Moorish ex-boxer called Ali, and when he arrived the four escapees pounced on him. There was a short struggle and Ali was overpowered. The noise, however, brought a near-by prison officer who was also quickly silenced. They removed his pistol, and tied and gagged them both. They then locked up some of the ordinary prisoners who did not want to escape to avoid compromising them in the attempt. An Italian who worked in the prison office and who knew what documentation was required to leave the prison was one of those involved in the escape. They edged into the office and easily overpowered the two auxiliary warders and one prison officer who were sitting playing cards. As it happened it was the same prison officer who had arranged Sabate's meetings with his wife. In the office they picked up another two pistols. Once they had tied up the three they made their way to the governor's office, where they found the governor, sitting talking to his French wife, who was pregnant at the time. Sabate, gun in hand, explained that he had no intention of using violence but that he was going to leave jail, and nothing or no one would prevent him doing so. Everyone was locked up in a cellar below the office. However, the most difficult part remained: to get through the armed guards at the entrance to the prison. For that one needed a special pass from the governor. They found the necessary papers in the office and Sabate took them to the governor.

'We know we're risking our lives, but that's a chance we'll have to take,' he said. 'Now sign this and don't try to fool us because we won't forget it if you do. Sign correctly and remember your life depends upon it.'

The governor signed. Everything went through without a hitch. One of the prisoners handed his paper to the officer on guard duty and no one stopped him. A few minutes later, Sabate and the other two did the same. They were free!

The escape was not discovered until the evening meal was being given out late that afternoon. The Regional Committee of the CNT was in for a surprise! Sabate was once again in Barcelona!

The two young Spaniards who escaped with him were sent by the Regional Committee to the 133rd Brigade of the 24th Division. (Later they deserted and were executed by the Communists before they could reach Barcelona.)

It was obviously necessary to take Sabate out of circulation for a time. If he were discovered again no power on earth could save him from a firing squad. He was advised to go to a children's colony on Masqueta, in the district of Igualada, which was run by the CNT under the care of a comrade named Batista Albesa, in whom they had complete faith. There he could remain for a time in complete security. Sabate agreed, but to avoid any incidents on the way decided to do the forty miles or so by foot. He went with his brother-in-law, Castells Marti.[13] Travelling by night the two comrades wandered into a gun-powder store without realizing it. There they slept for some hours. At daybreak, when they went to start their journey again, they realized they were in an extremely difficult situation. They noticed they were surrounded on all sides by barbed wire. Carefully they slipped out of the mouse-trap into which they had foolishly walked, but, after going only a short distance, a Carabinero patrol ordered them to halt. They were dirty, unshaven and wore leather jackets with their haversacks on their backs. Obviously they could not help but look suspicious to the patrol.

The Carabineros decided to take the two to the nearby command post – not without a great deal of protest on their part. For *El Quico* the situation was more than critical. If he allowed himself to be taken to the command post it would mean identification and certain death – about that there was no doubt. What could he do? Sabate tried to convince the guards to allow them to continue their journey and told them repeatedly they were on home leave and were returning to the villages but had lost their way in the dark. He protested so angrily to the Carabineros that one of them asked him for his papers.

'Naturally,' said Sabate, 'you should have asked us that first.

It was the question for which he had been waiting. Sabate opened his jacket, brought out his pistol, and shot the four carabineros before they knew what was happening. Once more he was free – the dilemma of killing or being killed had been resolved, but this time at the expense of four men carrying out their duties. It seemed as if Sabate was doomed to a life of trouble and violence. Even when he went out of his way to look for peace, trouble came looking for him. This time it was so great that even provisional refuge was out of the question. As they fled from the area Sabate remembered, too late, that he had left behind his haversack. Inside were a number of books he had bought from the Libertarian Bookshop in Hospitalet before leaving on his journey. In one of the books was a receipt made out in his name. He might as well have sent a written confession to the *Hijos de Negrin*.[14]

For greater security, the two separated, and Sabate once more set out for Barcelona. Whenever danger threatened, Sabate always put his faith in Barcelona. He left by train from a station near Martorell. This time, strange for one who usually took too many precautions, he was over-confident. He did not believe they would be waiting for him in the city so soon. Coolly, but alert, he got off at the *Francia* station. Walking along the platform, he saw a large number of police and security men examining their papers. He immediately dashed into one of the passenger coaches and out across the railway lines. However, he was spotted by one of the guards who gave immediate chase. He managed to shake them off by leaping on and off trains and across the tracks, but outside the station he saw they were sending out patrols to cut off his access to the city. Due to the scarcity of petrol, horse-drawn carriages were in vogue in Barcelona at that time. His lucky star shone on him, for at that moment one of the carriages drove by with passengers inside. He jumped in beside the coachman as it passed. The driver, a pistol between his ribs, passed the cordon thrown round the area with no questions asked.

This time *El Quico* managed to join, without further mishaps, the 121st Brigade of the 26th Division (Durruti) where he was amongst comrades, and able to resume the struggle against fascism. In the last few days of the war he took part in the desperate resistance at Montsech – winning the Medal for Valour – where entire sections were killed on the parapets as the enemy gunfire took its toll. With his division he travelled the length of the River Segre towards the Sierra de Cadi, where they intended to prepare a last-ditch resistance. This idea, however was rejected by the High Command and also by the Confederal committees, who were already making their way into exile in France.

On 10 February, 1939 the forces of the 26th Division

entered France through the Puigcerda sector. They were the last organized units to leave Barcelona. Sabate and his comrades of the Division were interned in the concentration camp of Vernat d'Ariege.

As we have seen *El Quico* was not the type of man to remain behind barbed wire for long, and at the first opportunity he made his escape. Strangely enough, however, this man who knew no fear nor accepted the authority of the State, did an unexpected thing. After wandering around in the Pyrenees, hungry and suffering from chest trouble, he returned voluntarily to the concentration camp – this time to the infirmary where he accepted his fate with resignation. France depressed him : 'You talk and talk and no one understands what you're saying, you hear them talk and you don't know what they're saying !'

[1] After the defeat of the rising, the Militia Committee was the only effective power in Catalonia. The Generalitat, although it still existed as the civil power in the province, was there in name only. The Militia Committee had representatives from the *Esquerra*, the Catalan Nationalist Party; from the parties of Republican Action; from the *Union de Rabassaires*, and from the Marxist parties (PSUC, United Socialist-Communist Parties of Catalonia – an amalgam of two parties both of which were, at the time, weak in that province; and the POUM, United Workers Marxist Party, a breakaway from the International Communist ideas which preceded the orthodox Communist Party, at one time with some sympathies with Trotsky); the CNT and the FAI.

[2] Vivancos was born on 19 April, 1895 in Mazarron (Murcia) and died in April 1972 in Cordoba, where he was on holiday.

[3] Jover was born in 1892 and died in Mexico in 1966.

[4] Jesus Hernandez, in his book *I Was Stalin's Minister*, says that seventy per cent of all control of the army was in the hands of the Communist Party. Decisive sections such as aviation and tank regiments were completely controlled by the Party.

[5] The United Young Socialists was a hybrid organization created by

39

Russian advisers in April 1936 bringing together the Young Communists, Socialists, and the Socialist Union and Proletarian Party of Catalonia. The leaders of this youth group, under the control of Moscow, were Trifon Medrano, of the Young Communists, who died in Bilbao in 1937, and Santiago Carrillo, of the Socialists, who, after becoming a Minister in exile, later became General Secretary of the Spanish Communist Party.

6 The Control Patrols were formed in Catalonia in August 1936 and were composed of men proportionately from the different anti-fascist organizations. About half were from the CNT. It was created to defend 'revolutionary order', but was dissolved by the Generalitat in March 1937, who gradually carried out a programme of disarming all the revolutionary organizations in the rear-guard in order to build up the armed bodies of the State.

7 On 20 December, 1917 an organization was formed in revolutionary Russia under the title 'Extraordinary Commission to Combat Counter-Revolution and Sabotage'. Before long this organization became known to the world as the 'Checa' – organized along the same lines as its Czarist predecessor, the Okrana, formed by Alexander II in 1880. It was the first police organization in the world to adopt a scientific approach in its investigations. The agents of the Checa arrested, tried and executed their own victims – almost always in complete secrecy. In 1922 the organization changed its name to the 'Political Department of State', better known as the GPU, and again in 1934, the name changed once more to 'Commissariat of Internal Affairs' (NKVD). The methods of this organization were introduced into Spain by Russian advisers during the Civil War. The Okrana, Checa, GPU, and NKVD were always one and the same organization – the only possible difference perhaps being that throughout the years it developed its terrorist methods against its political and ideological opponents into a fine art. For a long time after its change in title people continued to refer to it as the GPU. It was from this organization that the Nazis took their model for the Secret State Police (*Geheime Staats Polizei* – the Gestapo) under Herman Goering in 1933.

8 On 3 May, 1937, at three in the afternoon, by order of the Counsellor of the Government, Artemio Aiguade, a member of the Esquerra Party, a patrol of Assault Guards led by Commandante Eusebio Rodriguez Sales, Commissioner for Public Order in Catalonia and a member of the Marxist PSUC, attempted to take by storm the Barcelona Central Telephone Exchange, which was occupied and run by militants of the CNT-FAI. The anarchists resisted, and within a few hours Barcelona was a mass of barricades, open battle having broken out between the Anarcho-Syndicalists and the Communist-controlled State Forces. The PSUC militants allied themselves during these events with the official State body.

9 Fontanet escaped to France after the Civil War and later moved to

South America where he is now living.

[10] The SIM was formed at the instigation of Soviet advisers, on 15 August, 1937, at the same time as the Negrin Government set out to destroy the POUM – using its 'Trotskyite' tendencies (then a CP swear word) as a lever to destroy the libertarian movement and the anarchist-inspired collectives of Aragon as well. The constitution of the SIM was drawn up by Indalecio Prieto, a Socialist Minister in the Republican Government. Ostensibly its aim was to counteract the activities of the Francoist espionage service but, in reality, from the moment of its inception it was the executive arm of the Russian Secret Police, the NKVD, in whose cells many anti-fascists were tortured and murdered. The SIM aided the Communist Party at the front just as much as at the rear. Those who were impervious to its proselytizing were often physically eliminated. For further information on the SIM, see Jose Peirats: *La CNT, en La Revolucion Espanola*, Chap. XXXVI, Vol. III, Ed. CNT, Toulouse 1953.

[11] For further information on the role played by the Spanish Communist Party during the Civil War, and its crimes against the anti-fascists, see Rudolph Rocker's *Extranjeros en Espana*, Ed. Iman, Buenos Aires 1938; and Diego Abad de Santillan's: *'Por-que perdimos la guerra'*. Ed. Iman, Buenos Aires 1940.

[12] Augustin Remiro Manero was born in Epila, Zaragoza, on 5 August, 1905. He was a Centurion in the Durruti Column and later transferred to the 25th Division where he fought as a commando behind enemy lines. After the Civil War he escaped to France but was one of the first to return and dedicate himself to guerrilla activity against the Franco régime. He was arrested and murdered by the Francoist authorities – the date of his death is unknown.

[13] In September 1972 we located Castells Marti in Perpignan, but he was seriously ill and incapable of speech.

[14] Juan Negrin Lopez was a 'Moscow' man and tool of the Spanish Communist Party. He organized the Carabineros (100,000 men), who were called 'Sons of Negrin' by the people. Negrin was born in Tenerife, in the Canary Islands, in 1887, and died in Paris in 1936.

CHAPTER III

The Second World War

When World War II was officially declared on 3 September, 1939, one of the first consequences in France was the opening of the concentration camps in which the Republican Army languished after many months of inglorious battle against hunger, smallpox, lice and dysentery.

Thousands and thousands of Spaniards were incorporated in the production battle, generally in the factories involved in the war economy such as munitions, aviation, explosives, or in the associated activities such as the construction of dams and roads.

Some 50,000 'rojos' ('reds', as they were referred to), were organized on military lines into labour battalions. Others, after being examined as though they were in a slave market, were enlisted into the Foreign Legion or the Pioneer Corps, to be used as shock troops on the Eastern Front. Cannon-fodder was so abundant that the recruiting officers threw out anyone with a suspicious scar or even a bad tooth.

Sabate left the camp in December 1939 and was sent to the building site of a gun-powder factory at Angoulême.

The war did not begin in earnest for the French until 10 May, 1940. For more than eight months the two belligerent camps watched each other closely then, suddenly, everything happened at once. A hurricane of steel and fire swept over France. On 14 June German troops of the XVIIIth Army under Von Kuchler entered Paris, and, only thirty-six days after the offensive began on the Dutch frontier, swastikas flew over the Eiffel Tower and the Arc de Triomphe.

When the French Front disappeared, Sabate attempted to escape, but realized the German Panzers could move faster than he. He decided to adapt himself as best he could to the existing situation.

At first the victors set up the illusory 'free' and 'occupied' zones. The latter ran the full length of the Atlantic coast down to the Spanish frontier, where the first German units arrived on 27 June.

Sabate in the meantime took a job in a factory producing charcoal burners (for ersatz petrol), and in 1941 his first daughter, Paquita was born.

At about the same time the first Resistance groups, escaping the German labour camps, took to the mountains, and within a short time became known as the '*Maquisards*', '*Maquis*' or *franc-tireurs*. In the cities sabotage units were organized, but most of these were later wiped out by the Germans.

We do not know exactly what Sabate's activities consisted of during this particular period of clandestine struggle, but certainly he was directly involved with the Resistance movement from its inception.

On 10 December, 1942 two warehouses, full of explosives, belonging to the *Poudrèrie Nationale d'Angoulême* (National Gunpowder Factory), were destroyed in a daring act of sabotage. A number of Frenchmen were arrested on suspicion of having been involved in the explosions, and one of these men had in his possession a photograph of a group which included Sabate. Needless to say, this was the same gun-powder factory in which Sabate had worked on leaving the French concentration camp in 1939.

Once again, his tranquil interlude was over : Sabate, accompanied by his wife and child, moved to Perpignan in 1943 – not without difficulty as he had neither prospects of work awaiting him, nor papers. However, he was lucky enough to meet the Mayor of Prades, a good friend and sympathiser of the Spanish refugees, who got him the necessary papers.

This problem solved, Sabate realized he could take up the struggle once again. Here was the Spanish border staring him in the face. He vowed to himself he would renew the interrupted fight. How better than by establishing himself in this area?

Together with his wife and daughter, *El Quico* moved into the little village of Comes, north of Prades, which had been deserted for some time – the only other occupants being a Spanish family. From the start Sabate and his family were at loggerheads with their new neighbours and, after a short time in this unbearable atmosphere, Sabate decided to move once again and rented a small house in Eus near Prades.

He bought some plumbing tools and set to work doing minor repairs and household jobs in the small cottages of the Pyrenean foothills. This way he got to know every inch of the surrounding countryside in the region of Vallespir and later, for a short time, joined a group of resistance guides escorting refugees from occupied France into Spain. This enabled him to gain an intimate knowledge of the Pyrenean mountains and passes which he was later to use with great frequency. The main route he used through the Pyrenees, and which he came to know like the back of his hand, was that through Gerdana.

One day, while walking through the streets of Perpignan, he met an old friend from the 26th Division, nicknamed *El Roset*. This chance meeting proved to be a decisive one in Sabate's life, as it catalysed all his ideas, giving him a definite goal at which to aim. The spirit which had united these two comrades during the battle of Almudebar in November 1936, now united them in the clandestine struggle against the Francoist régime.

CHAPTER IV

Hopes

The first Congress of Local Federations of the *Spanish Libertarian Movement*[1] was held in Paris in May 1945. It was undoubtedly the most important working class gathering in the history of the Spanish emigration.

The two wings of the libertarian movement – those who were opposed to, and those who had supported, participation in the Republican Government during the war, appeared at last to have sunk their differences and agreed to dedicate all their activities to the struggle against Franco. In the months that followed a number of delegates were sent into the interior.

To escort the first delegation the National Committee nominated a skilled Aragonese guide, Antonio C.G., accompanied by Jose C. and Valero G. This delegation was made up of two comrades: Angel Marin Pastor (twenty-eight years) a member of the National Committee, and Lucio G. Francisco Sabate, Emilio C., Jaime Pares Adan (*El Abisinio*) and *El Roset* acted as bodyguards for the delegation on their way to the capital. The job of the commission was to set up a communications group to organize closer contacts between the Organization in Spain and the exile movement, under the National Committee of the Interior, whose secretary, at that time, was Cesar Broto Villegas. They arrived safely in Barcelona at the beginning of October 1945. Sabate's main reason for going to Spain on this occasion was to establish bases for future guerrilla activities in the Interior.

Having arrived in Barcelona without incident Sabate set about the task of establishing his own contacts in the city. The first meeting took place in the mountains of San Pedro Martir, just outside the municipal boundary of Esplugas. This meeting-place was known of old to the anarchist militants, having been used frequently for this purpose during the periods of Republican repression. Sabate arrived at the rendezvous armed to the teeth, with a submachine-gun, pistol and two hand-grenades. He informed the comrades assembled there that he had been entrusted with the task of reorganizing the areas of Alto and Bajo Llobregat, and also that he was preparing a number of actions for the near future. However, he continued, he did not want to compromise any of the comrades who were already on police files or under surveillance.

The local comrades, having heard what Sabate had to say, gave him a run-down of the infrastructure of the organization in the area : all co-ordination meetings consisted exclusively of a group of delegates and printed local clandestine editions of the confederal papers – CNT and *Solidaridad Obrera*. Sabate was also told the names of comrades murdered in the area by the fascists and the names of those responsible for their deaths.

In order to carry out his plans, amongst which figured prominently '*attentados justicieros*' (reprisals), the first thing Sabate required was money to buy transport and to hide the necessary arms and explosives, organize operational bases and set up an efficient propaganda printing and distribution service.

Together with 'the Abyssinian' and one other comrade, therefore, he carried out a number of robberies in his home town of Hospitalet. One of the first victims was Juan Panellas Torras, an extremely rich man. Another was Manuel Garriga Pugador, a well-to-do businessman who owned a large store in the Calle del Generalissimo Franco. After tying-up both Garriga and his wife, the three comrades took with them two typewriters, 30,000 pesetas and two sack-loads of food. Before leaving the premises Sabate left his victims a note which said :

> We are not robbers, we are libertarian resistance fighters. What we have just taken will help in a small way to feed the orphaned and starving children of those anti-fascists who you and your kind have shot. We are people who have never and will never beg for what is ours. So long as we have the strength to do so we shall fight for the freedom of the Spanish working class.
>
> As for you, Garriga, although you are a murderer and a thief, we have spared you, because we as libertarians appreciate the value of human life, something which you never have, nor are likely to, understand.

The next victim was one of the leading fascists of Hospitalet, a man by the name of Canary. Sabate and the comrades broke into his house at four in the morning and, after tying-up Canary and his wife, made off with 25,000 pesetas, a sack of beans and a sack of potatoes. Before leaving he left a note similar in style to the one already mentioned.

Following these initial 'expropriations', the name of Sabate became well-known and respected among the people in the streets, factories and the clandestine meeting-places.

Apart from sympathy, these acts also gave the group an initial capital of over 90,000 pesetas. Amongst other things handed over to the organization was one of the typewriters taken from Garriga's house. This found its way into the hands of Jose G., a member of a recently-arrived delegation from France, which had been escorted across the Pyrenees by the veteran guerrilla fighter, Francisco Denis, better known to his friends as 'El Catala'.

The group took great care in establishing themselves and preparing their plans, for their immediate enemy was Commissar Eduardo Quintela Boveda,[2] who led a highly-organized, efficient and ruthless intelligence service, and was capable of the most devious machinations.

The efficiency of Sabate's organization did not take long to show results. One of its most outstanding early achievements was the freeing of a group of prisoners carried out in conjunction with the Defence Secretary of the CNT Relations Committee, who was, incidentally, an Italian named Antonio Pereira.[3] The prisoners concerned were two comrades facing capital charges and who were about to be transferred to another prison together with a third man, a member of the Communist Party. With information obtained for them by another comrade, Victorio Gual Vidal[4] which proved exact in every detail, the group prepared their plan. Sabate, El Roset and El Abisinio, took charge of the operation.

The release operation took place on 20 October, 1945. El Quico and El Roset approached the two Guardia Civil escorting the prisoners, and when they drew level with them, took out their guns and disarmed the surprised Guardia. As they held them covered, El Abisinio remained at the wheel of a car parked a few yards away with a sub-machine gun, to protect the rear. Everything seemed to be going off smoothly, without violence, when suddenly one of the guards being watched by El Roset drew his pistol and aimed at Sabate. The latter hesitated for a moment – which could have cost him his life – but El Roset, quite calmly, fired at point-blank range and the guards fell, badly wounded. The other guard fled, abandoning his prisoners. The incident taught Sabate a lesson: never bandy words with a policeman or Guardia Civil, without disarming him first. Prisoners and liberators ran towards the getaway car in which El Abisinio was waiting. The nearby

Guardia Civil hearing gun-fire, came running and opened fire on the group. *El Abisinio* let off a few rounds from his sub-machine gun, which cooled the spirits of the guardians of public order. They turned and fled. The operation was a complete success, except that the third prisoner, the Communist, refused to follow his liberators and returned voluntarily to prison.[5]

The police were not hard put to discover the identity of the robber in Hospitalet. The victims were well-known to Sabate and he to them. Perhaps this was why he chose them to be his first targets. He never operated anonymously. His normal behaviour from then on was to approach his victim or victims and say the three magic words, '*Soy el Quico*!' (I am El Quico). It was sufficient to paralyse most people. Civilians and military alike offered no resistance.

From 30 October, 1945 onwards the Barcelona police began a wholesale campaign of repression, arresting many militants, amongst them Jose G., the recently-arrived delegate from France to whom Sabate had presented the typewriter taken from Garriga's house in Hospitalet. The custom was whenever a number of comrades were arrested each individual would admit responsibility for a part of the accused actions, thus reducing the total collective charge. Jose G., who confessed to ownership of the machine, could never have imagined what he was bringing upon himself. He was beaten-up unmercifully, but of course could give no explanation to the police concerning the origin of the typewriter, as he was completely ignorant of its history. Not that it would have done any good explaining matters to the police – so far as they were concerned, Sabate, delegations and the organization were one and the same thing.

It has often been argued that the activity of the armed urban guerrilla groups was counter-productive from a revolutionary standpoint as it invariably had disastrous consequences for the

49

political side of the organization dedicated to propaganda and industrial action. Such arguments have never been reasoned closely – what was undoubtedly disastrous was not the armed actions, but the deficient structure of the clandestine organization. This is a theme outside the scope of the present book but some points should be made, as it is relevant to the struggle being fought to this day – and not only in Spain.

The Spanish Libertarian Movement never adopted a clear and concrete position in the struggle against Franco, and neither did it attempt to separate the activities of the political and guerrilla wings within its ranks. People took part in the planning of guerrilla actions who had not the remotest intention of participating in the operations themselves; the 'legal' political organization (in France) controlled the formation of the armed groups – stubbornly ignoring the fact that within its ranks were to be found informers, charlatans and hypocrites of every shape and size; while the administration was in the hands of political bureaucrats – a lunacy of the highest order, even ignoring for the moment the obvious dangers such a situation could (and did) give rise to – as the 'committee men' had a predilection for inventing what they called 'methods of action' and 'activities' which led inevitably to inaction and inactivity.

These errors, briefly outlined above, cost the movement dear. They were paid for with the blood and lives of some of its most outstanding comrades. The members of the action groups argued continually but unsuccessfully, within the organization hoping to rectify this sorry state of affairs and create an autonomous resistance organization through which the men and groups involved could claim responsibility for their actions and avoid, among other things, the effects of repression felt by those comrades involved in propaganda and industrial action. The MLE, however, never compromised itself in regard to the

50

action groups – it had become a servant of legality in exile. Within the Spanish Libertarian Movement nothing was totally authorized and nothing totally condemned – the standing of the action groups within the organization was in a constant state of flux. For example, men who at any given moment belonged to the urban guerrilla groups could pass to occupy responsible positions within the organization, and vice versa. This problem, perhaps the most important of all, was never faced openly, in spite of the disgraceful events which resulted with increasing frequency as the years passed – bringing with them demoralization and confusion.

---

[1] *Movimiento Libertaria Espanol* (MLE) – the CNT-FAI exiles.

[2] Quintela, born 1891, joined the police service in 1917, and became known as the 'expert' on anarcho-syndicalism. He was one of the fourteen principal police chiefs appointed after Franco's victory. (See *Franco's Prisoner*, by Miguel Garcia, Rupert Hart-Davis, 1972.)

[3] Pereira's real name was Tommaso Ranieri. He was born in Naples on 29 March, 1908 and, was forced into exile in France in 1928 as a result of his activities in the Italian Libertarian movement. He moved to Spain in 1932 and, on the outbreak of the Civil War, he took part in the attack on the Atarazanas Barracks on 19 July, 1936 together with Durruti and Ascaso. For the remainder of the war he fought in the ranks of the Ortiz Column, and, following the Republican defeat in 1939, was taken prisoner in Alicante. He soon managed to escape from prison with the assistance of the local Organization, who supplied him with forged documents. At liberty he resumed the struggle, once again becoming Secretary of the Anarchist Defence Committee. He was arrested eventually in October 1945, but with the intervention of the Italian Embassy on his behalf, he was released after twelve months and deported to Italy. Pereira died on 16 March, 1969 in the Italian town of Ventimiglia.

[4] Victorio Gual was executed in Barcelona on 4 March, 1947, accused of having taken part in the attack on a car belonging to the industrialist Fado, a notorious Falangist, in Esparraguera in 1945. Fado had been responsible for the execution of a number of Catalan anti-fascists. When called on to stop, Fado – who was collecting his factory wages from the

51

bank at the time – drove on at high speed. Though the attacking group fired at the car, no one was killed or injured.

⁵ One of the released prisoners was named Ezequiel Balencil.

52

CHAPTER V

Confusion

Franco's 'National Liberation' was carried out with an orgy of blood – a murderer's fury which lasted many months. From Barcelona to Seville, from Corunna to Valencia and Madrid, the blood of the Spanish anti-fascists ran in the gutters. Night and day the execution squads worked full-time. One accusing finger was enough to send a man to his death. After this period of mass extermination there followed another, no less efficient and as arbitrary as the first, the Councils of War.

Probably the victors thought that in a 'civilized' country they should at least cover their crimes with a cloak of legality. It was, after all, the defence of Christianity they were celebrating. Where the mass outrages ceased they carried on with raids.[1] Eighty or a hundred people were often dealt with in the one swoop. It did not matter if the accused knew each other or not – most had never seen each other in their lives before they set foot in the courtroom. The prosecutor read out only the most outstanding deeds of the different accused and the sentence was always passed immediately – death!

How many Spaniards were murdered in this way between 1939 and 1942? The exact figure will never be known, although it must run into hundreds of thousands.[2] Then, tiring of so much bloodshed, the Falangists changed their tactics. They began to try persuasion. They went as far afield as France in search of likely material amongst the emigrés. By various methods, which included coercion, they strove to enlist militant working men into the so-called National Syndicalist Centre (CNS). They even had the effrontery to approach such men of integrity as Juan Peiro Belis[3] and Jose Villaverde,[4] who were both murdered when they refused to prostitute their principles by collaborating with the fascists. So it was not strange that they should attempt to do the same with men of less merit, and less dignity.

In this new phase the Franco police agents not only tried to incorporate militant syndicalists and those experienced in labour relations into the CNS; they also tried to force them to submit to the will of the authorities after giving them the impression that they would enjoy complete independence. This happened, for instance, with the founders of the so-called Labour Party, which drew its members from various sources including the CNT and the Syndicalist Party,[5] founded by Angel Pestaña[6] in April 1933.

Because of their record, their contacts and their knowledge of the medium in which they had been so active for many years, these men were a serious obstacle to the development of the revolutionary movement after the Republican defeat – the more so when they managed to gain control of the reins of the clandestine organization in Catalonia. Pretending to help comrades who found themselves in difficulty, they played a treacherous game which proved disastrous for the whole working-class movement. Their favours included the freeing of prisoners and the dismissal of pending cases. In this way they managed to convince some credulous people in the organization that they were sincere and doing a worthwhile job when, in fact, they were the despicable instruments of the Police Headquarters. In particular one should mention Eliseo Melis Diaz and Antonio Seba Amoros, whose activities in this respect were particularly vile.

Melis was an ex-militant from the Textile and Fabric Syndicate in Barcelona who had been active in the Shop Stewards' Committee between 1931 and 1935 and had often contributed articles to the confederal newspaper *Solidaridad Obrera*. He was intelligent and active but, though well-known, he had never occupied any important position during the Civil War. His later activity permits us to suppose that even then, in the years prior to the outbreak of the Civil War, he was in contact with the Directorate General of Security. At the end of the war Melis remained in Barcelona and very soon began to appear in public with Quintela. Nevertheless, he was still able to convince some guerrilla comrades that he was working for the benefit of the CNT from inside the Police HQ. He even managed to become Secretary of a clandestine Regional Committee and, when he was voted out of this post, continued to intervene actively in the organization by claiming to be a member of a fictitious anarchist group.

His main function was to gain the confidence of comrades in order that the police could break up the clandestine organization if ever they felt matters were getting out of hand. The Catalan Police should give eternal thanks to Melis – as a result of his work, the setting up of an efficient resistance movement was retarded for many years.

Quintela, who has only recently died, always preferred to see an embryonic organization of the CNT where he could be completely informed of its activities and new members; above all, to know the intentions of the members. The one thing that worried the Head of the Secret Political Police (*Brigada Politico Social* – equivalent to our Special Branch) was the formation of groups such as Sabate's which did not come under any control.

'The weekly union stamp doesn't worry me in the slightest,' he used to say.

Antonio Seba was another obnoxious character, though less

so than Melis. His principal activity – though that was quite enough – was to act as Melis's lieutenant, and he became at various times secretary of different Regional Committees in Catalonia. During the Civil War Seba was chief of the 153rd Mixed Brigade, or the 'Land and Liberty' Column, as it was known prior to militarization. With men of the 25th Division he helped to take Belchite and also took part in the battle of Segre in August 1938.

Antonio Seba, suffering from a bullet wound, fled from Barcelona to Valencia in February 1949 following a clean-up operation led by the *Los Maños* Group under Wenceslao Gimenez Orive. The wound was not particularly serious, but it made him understand that his reign was at an end.

This confused situation made life extremely difficult – especially so for an underground movement. The credit for finally clearing matters up must go to the Libertarian Youth, who had particularly bitter experience of the subject. One of the first Regional Committees of the FIJL, Iberian Federation of Libertarian Youth[7] was brought down completely in March 1943 thanks to Melis, and one of its members by the name of Pallarols[8] was shot on the 8th of the same month without any legal proceedings having been taken against him. Pallarols belonged to the Libertarian Youth of La Torrasa.

One thing that spurred on the young Catalans at this time was the organization in France, in 1945, of the Libertarian Youth in exile, who held their first National Congress in Toulouse that April. Immediately following this congress, some of the finest elements in the Catalan Libertarian Youth Movement returned to Spain to renew the struggle, many being subsequently killed or imprisoned. To conclude these pages on the position of the Libertarian Organization in Catalonia, and the confusion caused by certain elements, we may mention Angel Marin, a delegate from the National Committee in

France, whom Sabate accompanied to Barcelona. He was arrested in October 1945 and by agreement with Quintela, made contact with Melis. The result of this meeting was that in December, Marin left prison to go on 'outside business'. He was said to have escaped. In a circular from the National Committee – MLE in France, sent round to the Regional Committees in 1946, it was stated:

> For some days we have awaited with anxiety the arrival of the delegation sent to Spain. Once in the Interior we received news that the Franco Police had information as to its whereabouts, but, happily, they managed to avoid the Security Services and return without incident. Apart from meeting comrades and collecting information the delegation had the job of ascertaining the whereabouts of comrade Marin and delivering to him a letter from the National Committee, informing him that he should return to France without delay. The delegates were instructed that once they had found him in Spain, they should discover why he had remained in Spain and whether he intended to remain there permanently or not – basically in order to decide what should be done about him. They were also instructed to allow him the necessary money to return to France. This delegation has now returned and informs us they were unable to make contact with Marin without going through Melis and Seba. Knowing the relationship of these two with the police it would have been suicide to attempt this course of action.

Angel Marin did in fact return to France accompanied by another comrade, Juan Farre,[9] soon after this on 17 March, 1946. He was expelled from the National Committee and never again given any position of responsibility in the organization.

Another very similar case was that of comrade Evangelisto

Campos, a delegate sent by the MLE to Barcelona, in April 1945, to make preparations for the Youth Congress scheduled to take place in Paris that May. During a police raid on a Regional Committee meeting in Barcelona in March 1946, Campos was wounded as he tried to flee. Later, however, while in police custody, he made contact with Melis who arranged his 'escape'.

---

[1] *Sacas* was the name given to the process of taking prisoners out to be shot.

[2] Daniel Sueiro says in his book *Los verdugos espanoles* (the Spanish executioners), Ed. Alfaguara, Madrid 1971, that 'the official legal' publication recording all sentences, including death sentences, ratified by the Spanish Supreme Court, was suspended, for the first time since its founding in 1870, in March 1936 and was not published again until 1947.

[3] Outstanding Anarcho-Syndicalist militant born in Barcelona in 1887. During the Civil War he was Minister for Industry under the Presidency of Francisco Largo Caballero. He was extradited from France, where he had sought refuge, by order of the Pétain Government and returned to Spain, where he was executed in Valencia on 24 July, 1942.

[4] Born in Santiago de Compostela. Arrested within a few days of the outbreak of the fascist rising, he was offered the top post in the propaganda section of the Falange and its Youth Section, the JONS, in exchange for his life. He refused to accept this offer and was murdered at the beginning of September 1936 in the outskirts of Corunna.

[5] Sanches Requena was the leader of the new Labour Party. During the Civil War he had been Governor of Valencia. Shortly before the fall of Madrid in the last few days of the war, Col. Segismundo Casado Lopez, leader of the National Defence Council, appointed him Commissioner of Police for Valencia. The reason being that he was 'acceptable to the nationals' – according to Wenceslao Carrillo in *El Ultimo Episodio de la Guerra Civil Espanola.* (Toulouse 1945). Requena was arrested in Alicante following the Francoist victory and sentenced to death. His sentence was commuted and after a few years he was released on parole. He died in Valencia in November, 1946.

[6] Pestaña was born in 1886 in Santo Tomas de las Ollas in the province

of Leon. He was several times Secretary of the National Committee of the CNT and was one of the delegates to visit Russia in 1919, to decide whether or not the confederal organization should affiliate to the Red International of Labour Unions, formed after the Russian revolution. Later he moved away from anarchism to the Syndicalist Party, which he represented during the Civil War as Vice Commissar of the Army. He died in Barcelona in 1937. Pestaña's decision to form a political party perhaps had its origins in the frustration he felt at the failure of the revolutionary movements of December 1931 and of January/February 1932. He felt that the repressive strength of the State was increasing rapidly and the only method of attacking it with any probability of success was from within. This is referred to in Maximiano Garcia Venero's book, *Historia de los Movimientos Sindicalistas Espanoles*, Ed. del Movimiento, Madrid, 1961.

[7] The FIJL Anarchist Youth Organization, was created in Spain in 1932.

[8] This Pallarols should not be confused with his namesake Esteban Pallarols, known in the Underground as Riera, who was Secretary of the First National Committee of the CNT formed after Franco's victory. He was shot with another comrade, Mares, in March 1946. Another member of the same committee, Jose Cervera Bernell, was given a long prison sentence and died in Valencia in March 1955, when he had only a few months of his sentence left to serve.

[9] Parro was born in Barcelona in 1916. After the Civil War he escaped to France where, during the German occupation, he joined the Resistance escorting escaped POWs and refugees across the Pyrenees. Later, he took part in the liberation of Toulouse and, subsequently, became a courier for the Organization between France and Spain. His body was found by the French police on the night of 16/17 April, 1946, in a sack floating in the Midi canal. He was bound hand and foot and had a bullet in his brain. In his pockets were found documents suggesting that he was on a mission into Barcelona.

CHAPTER VI

Action

The first job undertaken by Sabate and his group was to seek out active supporters and collaborators, not only in Barcelona but in the surounding villages and along the whole length of the road between Barcelona and the French frontier. He began to organize bases in the mountains and the city which would serve as refuges for the comrades, and also as arms depots and supply posts.

It would be no exaggeration to say that between 1945 and 1946 *El Quico* got to know almost every tree in every village and mountain in Catalonia. In February of 1946, while he was in Barcelona, he received a telegram informing him that Leonor had given birth to twins the day before. Without losing a minute, he immediately set out to return to France. Despite the heavy snow – waist deep in places – he crossed the border by way of Bañolas and Coustouges, finally arriving in Perpignan where his wife was still in the clinic. One of the little girls died a few days later, but the second survived and was named Alba.

The Sabate family had moved to Marquixanes shortly before this, abandoning their home in Eus (between Prades and Vinta). Sabate remained a few days in the Rosellon capital and then moved with his family to their new home, La Clapère, on the banks of the River Tech, about two miles from Prat-de-Mollo.

Once settled in La Clapère, Sabate then rented a small *casa de campo* further up the mountainside on the opposite bank of the river, hoping thus to make access to outsiders a little more difficult. This small cottage was known to the local inhabitants as '*La Soranguera*', and it was here that *El Quico* organized his first operational base for his journeys across the frontier. To cover his clandestine activities at this base he rented a small nearby wood and arranged to have it worked by a group of five comrades. Sabate had the idea of building a commune on this spot, finding it amusing that it should be within rifle-range of Spain, but the attempts to fulfil this dream were in vain. The people he approached defrauded him completely and in the end he was forced to abandon the idea.

The organization took advantage of *El Quico*'s visit to France and asked him to undertake an important mission transporting a huge quantity of arms into Catalonia. On 21 April, therefore, he left with a group of comrades (all veterans who had endured their baptism of fire), amongst them Ramon Vila Capdevila. The material, which consisted of sub-machine guns, ammunition and explosives, was to be taken to a pre-arranged spot inside Spanish territory. It was then to be transported to the Geronese village of Bañolas where it would be kept by a comrade in whom they had complete confidence. The group of five decided to split up in Bañolas and meet later in Barcelona. Two of them left on the morning bus to Gerona on 25 April, while another two intended to leave by the same way that afternoon. Sabate himself was making his own way the following day in a lorry, with the arms carefully concealed under a tarpaulin.

The afternoon bus left Bañolas at two o'clock. As there was a fair that day the village was full of travellers, which made things easier for the group as, in a crowded street, they were less likely to be noticed. After lunch the three friends left the inn where they had been staying, Sabate chatting to one,

61

Ramon Vila following a short distance behind. As they made their way to the bus station, two Guardia Civil suddenly approached the first two comrades and demanded their papers, which were duly produced and handed over for inspection.

It is hard to say what aroused the suspicion of the officers, possibly it was because the papers were made out to persons from Logroño whereas these two had pronounced Catalan accents. They ordered the two comrades to accompany them to the barracks. Sabate began to protest while Ramon remained watching quietly in the background.

Some citizens gathered round, looking on at the argument with some surprise. One of the Guardia Civil, with less patience than his colleague, or perhaps deciding to end the argument once and for all by showing his authority, drew his pistol. Ramon Vila, whose eyes missed nothing, saw how the situation was developing and jumped forward, shooting the Guardia Civil, Jose Godo Garcia, dead on the spot. The second, who had been the more fervent in the discussion, had scarcely got over the shock of seeing his colleague killed when he found the barrels of three guns pointing in the direction he should take. He prudently took off like a rocket in the direction indicated, while the resultant panic in the market place allowed the three to make good their escape.

For what it is worth, it may be mentioned here that it was not Sabate who fired the fatal shot on this occasion (as was inevitably stated by the Spanish press), but Ramon Vila. To this fact the best witness would have been the Guardia Civil who ran for his life, but it was no doubt a matter of prestige with him to have his colleague's death attributed to the notorious Sabate himself, whom he later, no doubt, identified from photographs.

Ramon Vila and the other comrade took refuge in the mountains. Sabate returned, cautiously, to the inn, for he was still responsible for the material which lay in two large trunks now in Bañolas. Arriving there, he took with him a sub-machine gun and the necessary ammunition, hiding the rest in a pile of manure at the back of the tavern yard where dealers and small traders left their horses and carts. At night-fall he abandoned the inn and took refuge in a cottage belonging to a reliable and trusted comrade.

Bañolas was only a small village, at that time, of 6,000 inhabitants. The Police and Guardia Civil busied themselves furiously among the villagers, making individual and house-to-house searches, setting up patrols and road blocks. Above all, the Guardia Civil wanted to avenge the honour of the Corps.

Sabate managed to escape the search by a retreat in which he received, he said later, the biggest fright of his life. The woman of the house where he was hidden gave him some peasant clothes and a scythe, and, with the tool on his shoulder, he passed through the cordon of guards controlling the exits out of Bañolas. Beside him the woman walked carrying a large food basket in which was hidden the sub-machine gun. It was the first and last time Sabate went unarmed.

Meanwhile, the innkeeper, worried at the intensive activity of the police, and seeking to remove any possible suspicion from himself, went to the authorities to report the disappearance of a suspicious character who had been lodging in his premises. It was not such a bright idea as he thought because the police, realizing that the innkeeper's suspicions were probably well-founded and that the real bird had flown, decided to make of him the example they needed to vindicate their 'honour'. They put him through the most terrible tortures to make him confess, leaving him crippled for life. Meanwhile they ordered a search of the inn and discovered the secret cache of arms in the dung pile.

Sabate, in his peasant's disguise, continued on his journey to

Barcelona, while Ramon and his friend returned to France to report what had happened.

As a result of police enquiries following the incident in Bañolas, one of the comrades in Gerona was arrested. He had acted as go-between for the action groups operating in Barcelona, particularly with that of Sabate. We do not know exactly what led to his arrest, although previous events in Gerona suggest an explanation. It is certain that when Sabate accompanied the delegation from the MLE in October 1945, contact had been established in Gerona with a local resident. When he returned to France, the 'local' gave him a number of important documents which, apart from minor matters, gave the complete disposition of Franco's border troops. When these documents were examined in France it was discovered they had been typed on the machine belonging to Melis.

It does not take much imagination, therefore, to assume that the contact was being used – consciously or not – by the Barcelona informer. Naturally all relationship with the 'local' was cut off. However, it left a difficult problem, for this man now knew many things and, living in the same district, could not fail to know the identity of his successor. At all events the arrest of this successor was a major police victory. He attempted suicide, but was prevented from doing so. Subjected to extreme interrogation the police obtained from him the address of a house in Barcelona frequented by the Sabate group – a dairy in the Calle Santa Teresa. The house was placed under close surveillance, in order to identify everyone who came and went, with the object, at the appropriate moment, of destroying them once and for all.

With his customary caution, Sabate arrived in Barcelona on 2 May, having made the journey from Gerona on foot. He was unaware that the contact in Gerona had been arrested, and his first objective was to search out the comrades who had preceded him to the Catalan capital. For various reasons he was unable to meet them and so decided to call at the dairy to find out where they were.

On 7 May the woman who owned the dairy managed to inform Sabate that her place was under observation and that the police had probably identified some of the comrades who had called there, including *El Abisinio*, who had appeared the previous day. Sabate reflected on the consequences of the police knowing about the dairy. To prevent any comrades falling into the trap prepared for them he had to sabotage the machinery being set-up by Police HQ. Discreetly examining the neighbourhood of the shop he saw a group of four workmen who appeared to be holding a heated discussion amongst themselves. Calmly *El Quico* walked straight up to them. Still apparently preoccupied with their discussion, the four men started to walk towards Sabate. When he was only a few yards away from the suspicious looking group, he drew his Mauser pistol and pointed it at them as though he were about to shoot. It is impossible to describe the look on the men's faces as they turned and ran as if all the devils in hell were after them.

El Quico, being an excellent marksman, could have killed them all had he so wished, but was not given to gratuitous violence. Once it appeared they were safely out of range the disguised policemen turned and opened fire with their pistols, but Sabate did not want to get involved and disappeared hastily. The important thing now was to inform his comrades that the dairy was a death-trap!

As he knew, several members of the group had already been identified, including 'the Abyssinian'. He had been followed discreetly, and was in imminent danger as the police knew his address – that of his sister, who lived in Travesera de Gracia, near the San Pablo Hospital. Now, following their brush with

Sabate the police guessed that nobody would fall into the trap, so they decided to act swiftly before everything they hoped to achieve was lost.

The whole family living in the dairy was arrested, and it may have been through them that the police managed to discover the addresses of Sabate and *El Roset*. Normally the discovery would not have mattered in the least since, with his customary caution, Sabate did not set foot in the house again, even to collect his belongings. Unfortunately, however, the trail led ultimately to the downfall of *El Roset*.

El Abisinio was the first of the group to fall. On 9 May, 1946, as he was entering his home, the police shot him down in a hail of gunfire on his own staircase. Jaime Pares died without being able to put up the least show of resistance.[1]

Following the murder of Jaime Pares, 'the Abyssinian', another comrade was imprudent enough to pass the street where the dairy was situated and was immediately taken to the cells of Police Headquarters.

El Quico did not, of course, go home, but he kept a close watch on his house under the very noses of Quintela's men as they went in to prepare an ambush for him on his return. Sabate had the daring idea of meeting the police in an open fight. He went with *El Roset* to meet the MLE contact, at that time Antonio Lopez,[2] to ask him to join them in taking the house by storm and giving the police the fright of their lives. Lopez, sensibly, did not agree. He thought it suicidal and pointless, to which viewpoint Sabate and *El Roset* had to agree.

On 26 May Sabate and *El Roset* split up, as the former wanted to go to Hospitalet to see how his parents were faring. He knew that his brother, Jose, was about to arrive from Valencia. Jose had been in charge of a battalion in 1938 when the Republican Zone was cut in two, and at the final disaster had been taken prisoner in the fall Alicante. He had been detained in the concentration camp of Albatera and in the Cartagena Penitentiary. Finally he was released on 'provisional liberty', and wrote to his family saying he would like to visit them.

Meanwhile *El Roset*, despite innumerable warnings from Sabate that his house would certainly be under surveillance, decided to go home for a time. Quintela's men were waiting for him on his arrival, and took him off under close arrest.

Sabate knew how dangerous it was for him to go to Hospitalet, but he dearly wanted to see his brother again. Drawing on all his knowledge and experience of police methods, he examined carefully the surrounding area before finally going to the house in the afternoon. There was no one at home, so he scribbled a note to Jose, which only he would understand, and left immediately through the back door to spend the night under the stars.

Next day, at dawn, he looked round cautiously to avoid meeting anyone he knew and noticed some unusual activity in the vicinity of his home. He turned the first corner he came to hoping to get as far from the house as possible – and walked straight into the arms of the *Policia Armada*![3] It was impossible to retreat without arousing their suspicions, so he plucked up courage and like any good citizen walked past the parked police cars cheerfully whistling to himself. It was not until much later that he learned how close he had been to death that morning. The police had orders to shoot him on sight without warning, and, sitting handcuffed in one of the cars, *El Roset* and the Gerona contact were waiting to identify him. His parents' house had been closely watched, and it is possible he had been seen entering the day before. At all events, when Sabate passed the cars and buses packed with police, all guns were trained on him, his life hanging by a slender thread.

However, both the contact and *El Roset* courageously affirmed to their captors that the man passing was not Sabate.

The same day his father, while leaving for work, was stopped by the Policia Armada who used him as a shield to enter the house. This was to be a common occurence in the years to come.

Jose and Francisco, the two brothers, were reunited a few days later, in the mountains. *El Quico*, told Jose about his activities and present and future plans. Jose had to return to Valencia to clear up some personal matters, but promised his brother they would meet shortly in France and there discuss plans for future actions. A week later Jose arrived in France and gave himself over fully to the struggle.

In June 1947 *El Quico* met a childhood friend, Juan P., on a bridge near San Baudilio de Llobregat. The meeting was not fortuitous – Sabate had sent word to Juan that he would like to discuss some matters with him. Juan P. had only recently moved to the little Catalan town of Gava following the death of his only son. When *El Quico* explained that he had planned a number of projects which centred around Gava and required Juan's assistance the latter agreed to help him in everything necessary, and the two men went their separate ways having agreed to meet a few days later. Juan's house was situated some 300 metres from the Gava barracks of the Guardia Civil and it was here Sabate came a few days later to spend the night and the following day, a Sunday, with his friend and family. They could not discuss much on the Saturday night as Juan, who worked in the nearby textile factory, did not finish work until nearly midnight and his wife worked as a day labourer in the fields, the only person in the house when *El Quico* arrived being the fourteen-year-old daughter. However most of Sunday was spent in deep discussion. Sabate's plan was to isolate the village by cutting off all communications to the village, storm the barracks of the Guardia Civil for arms, and to rob the Bank of Vizcaya.

He also wanted to deal with some of the local fascist leaders who played an important part in the repression which followed the 'National' victory. Such a daring plan obviously required detailed information and it was Juan's task, together with other local comrades, to obtain this. The project was never carried out, however, as in July Commissar Quintela's right arm, Eliseo Melis Diaz, was executed and the resultant repression forced Sabate and his group to return to safety in France. The police also became suspicious of Juan P., who was on parole from prison, which caused him to seek refuge, together with his family, in France. The Gava plan was therefore shelved for the moment.

The nature of Eliseo Melis Diaz's activities has been described in previous pages. The idea of eliminating this informer had been discussed many times and approved by all the resistance organizations. In April 1945 three comrades had travelled to Spain to effect the assassination but were unable to carry it out as a result of warnings being leaked to the police. Manuel Pareja, another comrade from the action groups, also went into Spain with this sole objective in mind, and had it not been due to the intervention of Angel Marin (the MLE delegate who 'escaped' from police custody with the assistance of Melis), would have been executed.

Previous to this, in October 1945, the National Committee of the CNT led by Cesar Broto was arrested and the Committee which succeeded it, whose Secretary was Lorenzo Iñigo, was also arrested at the beginning of April 1946. The Secretary of the new National Committee of the CNT visited Pareja on two separate occasions, insisting that it was of the utmost importance that Melis be eliminated as soon as possible.

In March 1947 the Spanish Libertarian Resistance Movement in Barcelona (MLR) was formed with the idea of separating all organizational and propaganda activities from the purely guerrilla actions. From now on it was intended that the MLR should be the military wing of the Libertarian Movement. The idea came from the comrades in the 'Interior' and was agreed by a new delegate from France. Later, however, the movement in exile disagreed with this decision and disavowed their delegate. Nevertheless, the movement in Spain decided to act on its own initiative and received the support of many excellent and experienced comrades including the group of Manuel Pareja. This collaboration bore fruit.

It was decided that the mere elimination of Melis was not enough. They were convinced that there were more people, not only in Spain but in France, doing the same thing, quite unknown to anyone. A plan was prepared which, it was hoped, would help unmask the traitors inside the organization once and for all.

The operation was given the code name 'Plan H' and was perfected down to the last detail. At noon on 12 July, 1947 Manuel Pareja, Antonio Gil (better known as Antonio Sancho Agorreta) and another comrade, made their way into a café in the Plaza Buensuceso where Melis was playing billiards, in his shirt-sleeves. Pareja went up to Melis unnoticed and touched him on the shoulder, telling him to come outside and not to offer any resistance. Melis, who already knew through Angel Marin what Pareja's intentions were, put on a brave front. He collected his jacket and left the cafe escorted by the three men.

In the street Pareja told him briefly that, more than his life, he wanted all the documents and papers he had in his possession and he would go with him to collect them. Melis realized he was in a position from which there was no escape, the more so, when going into the street, he found that in addition to the three beside him there were another three comrades waiting, Pedro Adrover Font, known as *El Yayo*, Ramon Gonzalez Sanmarti,[4] and one other. Before they set out Antonio Gil wanted to frisk Melis but Pareja insisted that it was not necessary. Pareja hoped by this to convince Melis that if he handed over the documents his life would be spared. This was to have tragic consequences.

Melis was convinced that he was taking the last walk of his life, so he showed no resistance – but all the time waiting for the first opportunity to get out of his terrible predicament. Suddenly, as they left the Calle Elisabets (where Adrover and the others had joined them) and went into the Calle Montalegre, Melis pushed violently against his two captors, managing to escape through a doorway and up the staircase. Pareja rushed after Melis, but as he paused in the darkness, Melis – who was already on the stairs – had a perfect view of his silhouette. He drew out his pistol and fired in the narrow passageway hitting Pareja, who fell fatally wounded. He had the presence of mind, however, to fall face down, and crawled towards Melis, firing rapidly. Melis fell limply and Gil,[5] stepping into the doorway, delivered the *coup de grâce* to the traitor.

Meanwhile, the four in the street had placed themselves strategically to prepare for any eventuality and protect the retreat. Gil soon reappeared with the news that Pareja was badly wounded and would have to be carried. In seconds they hi-jacked a passing milk lorry, guns in hand, and ordered the driver out. Gonzalez took the wheel and the others helped Pareja aboard. They then drove off at high speed. Pareja had not lost consciousness but knew that his wound was mortal. He begged his comrades to kill him and save themselves, but this they did not have the heart to do. They took him to the Casualty Hospital where they left him in the entrance foyer in terrible agony.[6]

When Quintela heard what had happened, he gave immediate orders that Pareja's life was to be saved at all costs. This solicitude was not out of any humanitarian feelings but his desperate desire to question the wounded man. It was, however, in vain, for Pareja breathed his last before the duty surgeon had a chance to arrive.

Melis had given excellent service to the Spanish Police, but in the long run traitors are despised by everyone. His death merited only a few lines in the Barcelona papers, which did not even mention his name:

'In one of the streets adjoining the Calle Fernando (they even concealed the true name of the place where it happened) two men in a lorry shot a man passing in the street. He received a number of bullets in the body from which he later died. Notwithstanding the speed and surprise of the attack, he managed to fire on his aggressors before dying, wounding one of them. The wounded man's friends took him to the Casualty Hospital where they left him. They then fled.'

With the death of Melis the MLR made its first public statement, in a leaflet which announced its policy:

'In the future we shall reply to Governmental terrorism with people's terrorism. We shall answer the murderer's bullets of the uniformed gunmen with the pistols and machine-guns of the MLR. Men of the MLR will carry out sentence on all traitors as they have already done in the case of the notorious Elisio Melis of unhappy memory, on July 12th, at 13.00. hours, in the Calle Montalegre in Barcelona.'

This communiqué was signed by the Revolutionary Committee and was dated 1 August, 1947.

[1] He was born in Barcelona in 1910 and joined the Confederal Trade Union Organization at a very early age. When he was sixteen he joined the clandestine defence groups. During the Civil War he belonged to a transport unit of the Durruti Column, and was later transferred to the bodyguard of the Armaments Secretary of Catalonia, Eugenio Vallejo Sebastian.

[2] Thirty-one-year-old Antonio Lopez was arrested in Irun on his return to Spain following a mission in France in July 1946, together with Diego Franco Cazorla, twenty-six years old, better known as Amador Franco. Both were shot on 2 May, 1947 in the prison of Ondarreta. For more on Lopez, see Miguel Garcia, *Franco's Prisoner* (Hart-Davis).

[3] The Policia Armada, popularly known as '*Los Grises*' ('the Greys'), were created in March 1941 to form an integral part of the Governmental Police. Their mission was simple – public order and repression. The Corps is organized on military lines with infantry, cavalry and motorized divisions. Supreme command is held by the military general based in Madrid with the title of Inspector General. The day-to-day running of the Corps is managed by the Directorate General of Police, Civil Governors and local Police Chiefs. According to the official statistics for 1971 the Corps is made up of 52.28% workers, 39% country labourers and 8.44% students, numbering at the present time 100,000 men.

[4] Born in Granollers in May 1920, died in Barcelona July 1948 during a gun-battle with the police.

[5] Antonio Gil was born in Urrea de Jaen (Teruel) January 1921. He died in Toulouse in a lorry accident in April 1948.

[6] Pareja was born in Velez Rubio (Almeria) in 1910. During the war he was Commissar of the 104th Brigade.

CHAPTER VII

Problems in France

The Spanish Libertarian Movement in exile celebrated the IInd
Congress of Local Federations in Toulouse from 20 May until
29 October, 1947. This meeting was attended by many activists from the Interior, including Jose Lluis Facerias and Francisco Sabate. Also attending were representatives from the
MLR, but these were refused delegate status by the Congress
bureaucracy and not allowed to participate in the heated
discussions concerning the future role of the Libertarian Resistance movement in Spain.

As usual, the Congress ended with a call for greater militancy and a more dynamic propaganda and action campaign
in Spain – completely meaningless, but necessary to placate the
demands of the always more militant rank-and-file of the
movement. Certainly the bureaucracy even went so far as to
refuse to permit the wishes and comments of the guerrilla
groups being heard or discussed while the Congress was in
session.

Disgusted with the manoeuvres of the bureaucracy, Facerias
prepared to leave France with his group and return to Spain.
Francisco Sabate, Alberto B., and another comrade had pre-
pared the ground for this trip by setting up an arms cache for
'*Face*' in the Mas Tartas base near Osseja in the French
Eastern Pyrenees. The three comrades had transported all the
arms and explosives to Osseja from the main arms dump in
Font Romeu.

Facerias was taking with him a special delegate from the National Committee of the CNT (whom we shall refer to as C) but unfortunately, before they crossed the frontier, they were arrested by the French border guards near Latour de Carol and taken to Perpignan prison. Unexpectedly, however, the group was released after fifteen days without any trial or court appearance whatsoever and, undaunted, renewed their preparations for the journey before the winter snows made it impossible. The journey turned out to be dogged with ill-luck.

The group was guided by the veteran anarchist militant Mariano P. Unfortunately, as they were packing the material to be taken with them, a hand-grenade pin came loose and blew up in Mariano's hand as he fumbled with a locked shutter-catch, trying to throw it out of the window. A fragment from the grenade hit Ramon Ballester Orovitg, wounding him in the knee. The comrades carried Mariano to a doctor in the nearby village of Osseja where his wounds were dressed and, as he required surgery, he was then taken to Perpignan hospital, where his left forearm and thumb of his right hand were amputated.

Eventually the group, consisting of Facerias, Ramon Gonzales, Celedonio Garcia Casino and Rafael Ballester Orovitg left for Spain on 6 December. Bad luck continued to follow them, however, for Rafael was forced to return to France due to an infection in his wounded knee.

At the same time as these events were taking place the Sabate family moved from La Clapère to another casa de campo near Coustouges. This house was even better suited to his plans, being only one kilometre from the frontier. To keep Leonor and the children company during his many absences he brought with him a young comrade to do the odd jobs around the house and to look after the land. He also bought a mule, which proved to be of inestimable value in helping with these chores. His labours were observed with some irony by the neighbours -- though at a distance, the nearest house being over half a mile away as the crow flies. To buy seeds and other materials he had to travel to Ceret, Arles-sur-Tech, St Laurent and even as far afield as Perpignan, and everyone he met he tried to fire with enthusiasm for his dream of a libertarian commune in that pleasant area. The people of the area knew -- or at least thought they knew -- that particular piece of land only too well. They looked on his hopes with scepticism. Others, they said, had tried in that same spot and failed miserably.

However, *El Quico* was not only stubborn, he was a man of initiative and a hard worker. He got hold of an old pump and -- always accompanied by his mule -- dug the necessary ditches and even managed to get water up to the house. To the amazement of his detractors the make-shift farmer was soon producing melons the like of which had never been seen before on the French slopes of the Pyrenees.

At about this time, however, an event occurred in France whose repercussions were to be intimately linked with Sabate's later life. On the night of 6/7 May, 1948 a number of masked and armed men arrived in a car at the yard of the Rhône Poulenc factory in Peage de Roussillon (Lyons) with the intention of robbing the payroll. They cut the telephone wires and bound and gagged two of the guards, Poncet and Hennebaud. The third, Maurice Monnot, who was on his rounds at the time, opened fire in an attempt to stop the robbers, and was killed in the ensuing gun-fight.

The unintended death of the guard forced the robbers to leave the factory immediately and make their escape in the car they had arrived in. The escape was made in such disarray and panic that they left behind them a vast number of clues.

The robbers had changed the number plates of the car, and, for some reason, no doubt to change them again when they had made good their escape, when they got out of their car on arrival the number plates were left lying on the ground. In their sudden haste to escape they forgot them.

The police identified the owner of the car number 7263 FS8. It was registered in Haute Garonne as belonging to a Spaniard by the name of Carlos Vidal Pasanau, a resident of Toulouse, who had bought the car in November 1947 from a garage in Toulon. Vidal was in Spain and could not be interviewed by the French police.

On the night of 15 May, 1948 on Route Nationale 115, near the village of La Cabanasse in the district of Ceret in the Pyrenees (only a few miles from the Spanish frontier), French Customs officers carried out a 'stop and search' operation. As they were asking the passenger of a taxi they had stopped to get out to produce his papers, the man gave them a sudden violent shove as he handed over the documents and ran off into the night. The Customs officers fired a few shots, but without hitting anyone. The documents the man dropped were in the name of Francisco Sabate Llopart. Inside the taxi they found an automatic pistol.

A few hours later Customs men raided the *Mas Casenove Loubette*, the Sabate home. They searched the premises in the presence of Leonor and found two American portable radio transmitters and receivers. These were confiscated as contraband, something which was sorted out satisfactorily between the Customs and Sabate after a year's discussion. However, on 21 May, a few days after the first visit Police Commissioner Dupouy came to effect a more meticulous search and found a sack containing: a packet of twenty-two cartridges of explosive material; five hand-grenades; three metal tubes packed with explosive substances; fourteen light bombs;[1] two bombs described as dangerous, and two boxes each containing fifteen detonators.

After making his escape from the taxi as described, Sabate managed to cross the River Tech and hide for a few days in the house of a friend who lived quite near. He did not travel far as he was shortly to take a group of nine people (including himself) into Spain, amongst whom were his brother Jose, Ramon Vila Capdevila and Francisco Martinez Marquez. Sabate, who was in Spain at the time, was charged in his absence with illegal possession of the arms and explosives found in the *Mas Casenove Loubette*. The case was heard in his absence by the Ceret Correctional Tribunal on 23 November, 1948, and *El Quico* was fined 50,000 francs and sentenced to three years imprisonment.

On 12 January, 1949 a number of libertarians, arrested the previous May, were released from prison in Spain. Amongst these was Francisco Ballester Orovitg. During his imprisonment Ballester had prepared a census of all the CNT detainees, with the addresses of the families and the names of the lawyers who had defended them. The purpose was to organize in as efficient a manner as possible material aid for the prisoners, their families, and supply them with legal aid. To prepare this project he got in contact, through an intermediary, with Sabate, whom he knew quite well.

The idea of organizing help for the prisoners was taken up by Sabate with great enthusiasm as it had been one of the problems which had worried him consistently. He asked his brother Jose – who was at that time in Barcelona – to work with Ballester to prepare a realistic plan of action. With this done, Jose and Ballester approached a sympathetic lawyer to take charge of the legal aid for prisoners. Sabate's group undertook to cover all expenses involved in the project, without any help from the MLE.

As usual it was a question of money. Once more, the activist groups had to fall back on the banks for forced contributions, they had no other source of income and it was for this reason that robberies played an important role in the Resistance movement.

Here we include some of the more important acts of expropriation which took place during this period of our story:

28 January – Textile factory of *Jose Sanglas* in Avia, Barcelona, amount taken, 65,000 pesetas.

18 February – Branch of the *Banco Central de Barcelona*, amount taken 77,000 pesetas.

23 February – *Sociedad Anonimo Ferrero*, Barcelona. (The Director of this firm, Jose Ferrero, was shot dead when he attempted to prevent the robbery.)

Jose and Francisco, together with Jose Perez Pedrero, called *'Tragapanes'* because of his continual hunger, and another comrade planned a 'political prisoners operation' against a bank near Barcelona, the Gava Bank, which Sabate knew well – he had robbed it successfully as far back as 1935! Although this particular attempt failed it does illustrate the reason for Sabate's survival throughout many years of constant action. It was due not only to his courage and character and a certain amount of luck, but to his extreme caution at all times. He was daring but never suicidal.

This bank had managed to foil any further robbery attempts after 20 January, 1949 because, due to the large number of bank raids, all banks in Catalonia were supplied with two armed police who stood guard in the doorway. Sabate had tried to raid it once before, but, finding the risk too great for two men on their own, he called it off. The reason this attempt failed was due to different reasons. Jose and *Tragapanes* had stolen a car for this job a few hours before the deadline. Jose, who knew how meticulous his brother was regarding time –

particularly in something of this nature – had let the owner of the car go free, although he knew the man would go straight to the police. There would still be enough time to do the job successfully.

This time, owing to circumstances completely beyond his control, *El Quico* and his friend arrived in Gava by taxi much later than expected. When Francisco heard at what time the driver of the stolen car had been freed he decided to leave the robbery for another day. This was certainly a stroke of luck! As the four returned to Barcelona, the car broke down after travelling only a few hundred yards. All their efforts to fix it were in vain. Had this happened after the robbery, perhaps even when they were being followed, they would have been in a very tight spot.

Unknown to Ballester, however, he had been under close surveillance by the police since leaving prison. Through following him they were able to track down the address where Sabate was staying, and hoped to lay hands on not only his group, but all the other action groups as well. The police plan failed because of the prudence already mentioned and the experience gained from clandestine struggle. Nobody, for instance, came or went to Sabate's house, or anywhere for that matter, without first taking great care to check that the place was not being watched by the security services.

For this reason Ballester immediately spotted the police and realized the danger he was running. He conferred with Francisco and Jose Perez Pedrero, and together they decided to teach the police a lesson. Arming themselves to the teeth, they made their way to the house in Sans, where the trap for them had been set. When they got there, however, the three policemen Jose had seen earlier had disappeared. Instead there were two well-dressed gentlemen walking up and down the street. Were they a relief? It was up to them to answer. *Tragapanes* and Jose hid discreetly to give covering fire if necessary, while Francisco walked up to the strangers. He produced the Thomson sub-machine gun which he always carried under his raincoat and asked for their papers.

The two men, surprised, handed over their documents. One was a pharmacist and the other something similar. They might well have been ordinary citizens, but it was also more than likely they were undercover agents. Francisco told them to get out of the district immediately, and warned them that if he set eyes on them again he would not waste time asking for papers.

The incident came to the attention of the police, who realized that further surveillance of the house was a waste of time. They went to the lawyer instructed by Ballester, with the intention of gaining information that would lead them to the group, but he could tell them nothing. The only person he had been in contact with was Ballester.

The police, now afraid that even Ballester would escape from their clutches, ordered his immediate arrest. He was taken into custody by the Brigada Politico Social, to the cells of their headquarters in the Via Layetana in Barcelona. It was difficult for Ballester to deny any knowledge of the Sabate group as the police had a full record of all his movements from the moment he left the Model Prison. Naturally, what they wanted from him was the place and date of the group's next meeting. Ballester had no way out. Under torture he admitted that his next rendezvous with the group was on 26 February in the foyer of the *Cine America*, in the Avenida del Marques de Duero, No. 121, at 6.45 in the evening, or, in the event of a slip-up, at No. 91 on the same street, which was the *Cine Condal.* Ballester[2] had used a ruse, however, which managed to sabotage the police manoeuvre, although it could have had tragic consequences. He told the police that his contact with the group was through Francisco Martinez (*Paco*), a man already known to the police. Thinking they were dealing only with the arrest of Marquez, they took precautions, but not in any way as much as they would have done had they known they were dealing with the Sabate brothers.

The strongest police guard was around the *Cine America*, which Ballester had given at the first rendezvous, directly under the orders of the Chief of the *Brigada* himself, Pedro Polo Borreguero,[3] a man notorious for his persecution of anarchist militants. Previously he had been the confidant of Miguel Badia,[4] the Catalan Chief of Police who, with the complicity of the Republican Government, re-enacted the police terror carried out by Severiano Martinez Anido and General Miguel Arlegui y Bayones.

The Special Services Brigade was formed in September 1946 to reinforce the *Brigada Politico Social* and Polo, at that time second in command of the BPS, was appointed its Supremo. Polo thus acquired the same rank as Eduardo Quintela, Chief of the Social Brigade. Both brigades came under the control of the Police Commissioner, Manuel Chinchilla.[5]

That night it so happened that the Sabate group intended leaving for Martorell, and in order to waste as little time as possible, they went along together to the meeting with Ballester, not knowing of his arrest. Before the arranged time of the rendezvous a policeman, Oswaldo Blanco Gregorio, was posted in the foyer of the *Cine Condal* while Inspector Jesus Martinez Torrecilla and another policeman (Alvaro Varela Guillen), were respectively positioned at a street corner and a nearby garage.

Sabate's group approached the meeting place with the two brothers leading and the other two comrades following at a discreet distance. Jose, always attentive and alert, recognized Oswaldo Blanco from a distance – he was one of the two policemen keeping watch on his home address in Sans.

Jose warned Francisco of the danger and together they worked out a plan of action. Between the comrades and the cinema itself there was a newspaper kiosk which could act as a screen. Each would jump out from either side of the kiosk, capture and disarm the policeman, leaving him with a 'greeting card' for Polo.

Somehow Jose got in front of his brother and was immediately recognized by Oswaldo, who drew his pistol to deal with his quarry. At that moment Francisco came round the other side with his gun already drawn and, seeing the danger his brother was in, opened fire at point-blank range, hitting Oswaldo in the head.

Just as these events were taking place the cinema emptied. It is impossible to describe the panic – more so when the other plain-clothes man outside the cinema saw his colleague fall dead and the Sabate brothers with guns in their hands. He ran across the road, taking refuge behind a pile of rubble from nearby road works and began firing wildly at everything that moved. It could have injured a number of innocent victims, but luckily his shots went wide of all targets. Although he was well protected by the earth works, the policeman was finally silenced by a bullet in the thigh from Jose's gun. The brothers removed Oswaldo's papers and pistol, then made their escape through the screaming crowd before reinforcements could arrive.

Later, when the group met again, one of the other two comrades, who lived nearby and who had vanished during the fighting, said that when the battle began he realized he had forgotten his pistol . . . so he ran home to collect it ! The other went over the hill.

[1] *Petardos* as these bombs are called, are high explosive substances pressed in the shape of a geometric prism. They have a rectifying hole for the insertion of a detonator.

[2] Ballester, born in Barcelona, 12 September, 1920, was a fervent Esperantist. He later managed to return to France where he died in 1957, when the Paris/Nîmes Express crashed.

[3] Polo, born September 1897, joined the police force in 1921. During the Civil War he served in the Republican Zone as a servant of the Generalitat. Jose Peirats, in his book *La C.N.T. en la Revolucion Espanola* (Toulouse 1952), says that Polo was working for Franco's espionage service based in France. Polo died suddenly in December 1972 in Barcelona. Having retired from police service some ten years before, he was honorary Principal Commissar for Barcelona. Until the time of his death he was Chief of the Information Bureau for the Civil Government.

[4] Miguel Badia was assassinated with his brother, a main organizer for the fascist gunmen squads, in Barcelona's Calle Muntaner on 28 April, 1936.

[5] This new police organization was inspired by a similar service created by General Miguel Arlegui, Inspector General of Public Order, in Barcelona in 1920, together with his close colleague in the Civil Government of Catalonia, Severiano Martinez Anido. This organization was also called the Special Services Brigade and was led by Police Inspector Antonio Espejo Aguilar. The most significant difference between the two epochs was that Inspector Espejo did not last long in his new job. He was assassinated at the corner of Calle Regonir in the south of the city on 19 January, 1921.

CHAPTER VIII

Terror in Barcelona

Towards the end of February, 1949 Jose and Francisco Sabate came into contact with another action group – 'Los Maños'. The organizer of this group, which operated mostly in Barcelona, was Wenceslao Gimenez Orive. It is worth recording the circumstances in which they met.

The 'Los Maños' group had decided to get rid of the Barcelona Commissioner of Police, Eduardo Quintela, once and for all. They kept him under constant surveillance and carefully recorded all his movements, waiting for the most propitious moment to strike. Sabate's group, unaware of what 'Los Maños' had in mind, decided on a similar course of action. Quintela usually passed through the Calle de Marina on his way home from Police Headquarters at lunchtime and in the evening, and it was in that same street where the Sabate and 'Los Maños' groups met. After exchanging greetings and a few words it dawned on them that both groups had the same intention. Comparing notes at a joint meeting shortly after they found that their information coincided. Every day, with very few exceptions, Quintela left Police Headquarters in the Via Layetana to return to his home in the Calle La Vina, situated in the suburb of Guinardo, passing through the Calle Marina between 1.45 and 2.10 pm. This daily journey was made in his grey-coloured car, which carried the official insignia of his office. The two groups decided to lose no more time in discussion and arranged the time and place for the *attentat* to take place – between the Calles Mallorca and Provenza on 2 March, 1949.

In the early morning of the day fixed for the assassination 'Los Mañós' went to find a car (this turned out to be a Fiat belonging to a gentleman from Lorca who had arrived that day to carry out some business arrangements in Barcelona). The wheel was taken by Simon Gracia Fleringan and the frightened owner was made to sit beside Wenceslao in the back of the car. The three drove off to meet *El Quico* – who had by this time hi-jacked a truck – at a pre-arranged spot. The gentleman who owned the Fiat was considerately but firmly tied, gagged and put in the back of the truck accompanied by the Sabate brothers, while another comrade took the wheel. Jose Lopez Penedo, of Sabate's group, sat next to Wences in the Fiat and each car proceeded to the meeting place.

At 1.45 pm they parked the truck in the Calle de Marina, about a hundred yards from the church of the Holy Family. One man sat in the driving seat and another, in blue overalls, inspected the engine with a preoccupied air. The mechanic who seemed so absorbed with his engine was in fact watching carefully from the corner of his eye a young man in a brown hat, who was strolling up and down the pavement fifty yards along the road. The man in the driver's cab was Jose, the other, in overalls, *El Quico*.

About twenty yards further up the street the other three comrades were sitting in the parked Fiat – Simon at the wheel, Jose Lopez Penedo and Wences in the back with their Sten-guns hidden from view, but ready to open fire at a moment's notice.

At 1.55 the man strolling on the pavement ostentatiously removed his hat. The grey car, so anxiously awaited, was approaching the comrades along the Calle de Marina. *El*

Quico removed his machine gun from the open engine compartment and moved out into the middle of the road, balanced himself with his legs wide apart and opened fire on the approaching car. Riddled with machine-gun bullets, it screeched to a halt and two men jumped out in a vain attempt to escape. The Fiat drove forward and the occupants opened fire on the running men. Sabate, with gun on hip, ran to the bullet-torn car to check the identity of the victims. Quintela was not there! Despair was written across Sabate's face – the carefully prepared attempt had failed.

Inside, instead of Quintela and his usual bodyguard, were two Barcelona Falangist leaders travelling in the passenger seats – Manuel Pinol Ballester, Secretary of the local University Youth Front, and Jose Tella Bavoy, Sports Chief of the same organization. Pinol and the chauffeur, Antonio Norte, were killed outright, but the other man was only slightly wounded and was allowed to escape with his life.

These victims saved Quintela and only he can answer the many questions raised by this frustrated attempt. An identical car had travelled along the same street at the same hour every day with Quintela inside. Why had he changed his routine – was it an accident or a personal security measure? Did he know he was sending these men to their deaths? The answer to this mystery lives with Quintela. Perhaps some day he will reveal it in his last confession.[1]

The Falangist press followed the police initiative in referring to these as 'innocent deaths'. Certainly they were the wrong victims, but it should be remembered they came from a hierarchy which qualifies for any description but that of 'innocent'!

The attempt on Quintela's life in the Calle de Marina by the Libertarian Resistance had wide repercussions on the life of Barcelona. Not only in the capital, but throughout the province the police declared a state of war against the organized working class. Not only were there house raids, but the guardians of public order broke up groups of people in the street to such an extent that it became impossible to put on shows or entertainments in the evenings. After 8.00 pm the only people to be seen on the streets of the capital were patrols of the Policia Armada. The *Brigada Politico Social* felt itself powerless to guarantee order in the city and fell back on the Criminal Brigade, mobilized the Guardia Urbana and sent to Madrid for reinforcements from the Directorate of State Security. During this period the police patrols employed a fleet of fifty taxis with policemen inside, the hire sign still showing free. Everyone who hailed a cab was taken to Police Headquarters to have their papers checked. In fact this was a greater blow to the Resistance groups than it seemed – the taxi was their normal means of transport.

Such was the tension in the city that on many occasions there occurred terrible accidents. The police were so nervous they often shot peaceful citizens raising their hands to remove their identity papers from their inside pockets. Buses were stopped in the streets by patrols of five policemen who would search the passengers menacingly with guns in hand.

The action groups made no attempt to de-escalate the tense situation – in fact they did exactly the opposite. Wenceslao Gimenez, together with Simon Gracia, hi-jacked a private car and from it machine-gunned two policemen on guard duty in the centre of Barcelona in the middle of the day. Here is the official police communiqué issued to the press :

At 10.30 am., yesterday morning a private car drove along the Calle Provenza in the direction of the Paseo de General Mola and stopped outside the *Banco de Vizcaya*, situated at the junction of the above mentioned streets. Shots were fired from the passenger seat of this car at two officers of the *Policia Armada* on guard duty at the bank. This cowardly attack was successfully repelled by the police officers concerned but, however, the would-be murderers managed to make good their escape. Police officer Manuel Rodriguez Carballeda was seriously wounded in the attack and had to be taken to the *Hospital Militar del Generalissimo* where he was operated on successfully. His colleague was not seriously wounded however and was allowed home within a matter of hours. A passing pedestrian, Concepcion Fermens Queralt, was also wounded in the attack.

What was not mentioned in the press hand-out was the fact that the wounded woman was shot by the police as they repelled this 'cowardly attack'. The Commissioner of Police in Barcelona received an anoymous note about this time informing him that he was to be executed and that the Police Headquarters would be blown-up. The authorities took this threat seriously, believing it quite feasible, and reinforced the guard on the building – going so far as to have a permanent guard in the nearby sewers running under the Via Layetana.[2]

In addition to this no cars were allowed within a fifty-yard radius of Police Headquarters, and the police were under orders to shoot at any suspicious-looking vehicles. In some parts of the city there were large traffic jams while police stopped and searched vehicles and pedestrians at random. Finally, to prevent the blowing up of Police Headquarters, they squeezed into its cellars all the arrested anti-fascists they could lay their hands on. During the period of the alarm, which lasted some weeks, the Commissioner spent the whole time in the '*Jefatura*' without once going home. Many senior officers followed his lead and when they did dare to venture out they embraced each other, making their farewells as if never again would they meet – at least in this world. It was a time of complete panic.

At 2.00 am on 9 March, 1949 two taxis stopped outside No. 40 Calle Sanjurjo. Four Special Branch officers from the police station of Hospitalet de Llobregat, amongst them Policeman (Third Class) Antonio Juarez together with four Policia Armada got out of the two taxis and, after a few words with the night patrolman who had called the police, took up positions as though they were about to attack a fortress. One pair of the Policia Armada and the night patrolman covered a door of the house and the other pair covered the back. The four policemen went silently into the house, up to the first floor, where they knocked on a door.

The flat belonged to a railway worker, Angel Hernandez Rodriguez, who was at that particular moment working on the night-shift. The time of night and the number of police officers present indicated that this was not just an ordinary raid but was a special operation for a specific purpose. Somehow the police had discovered that members of the Resistance lived there. The railwayman's wife, Manuela Valerio Ramos, answered the door.

'Who's there?'

'A telegram.'

She opened the door and was confronted with the barrel of a gun. A voice whispered.

'Police! Who's sleeping in this house?'

'Two men,' she answered, shaking with fear.

'Where?'

She indicated the first room in the hallway and the four policemen entered the flat, guns at the ready.

Although the conversation was held in a whisper, the knock on the door awakened Jose Sabate, who had been sleeping in the rooms pointed out to the police. The door was slightly ajar, and Jose had witnessed the whole scene. When he saw the police approach he opened fire through the crack in the door. Antonio Juarez, who was in front, fell dead with a bullet in his head. The other three policemen panicked and fell back, rush-

90

ing out onto the staircase landing. *El Quico's* brother and Jose Lopez Penedo, who had been sleeping in the adjoining room, took advantage of this, and both made their way into the kitchen, which commanded the entrance to the flat. They overturned the kitchen table to use as a barricade and prepared to sell their lives dearly with what little ammunition they had left.

The police, without offering them the chance to surrender peacefully, opened fire from the landing. Jose Sabate was wounded by a bullet which passed through his chest and out again through his back, near his right shoulder. The two comrades realized that they had an impossible position to defend. They had to leave before police reinforcements arrived – something they knew would not take long. In stockinged feet they jumped out of the window into the street below. The two guards posted outside had moved off a little when they heard the initial shots, but not so far they could not see the two shadows making off down the street. They immediately gave the alert and set off in pursuit. Jose Penedo was brought down in a hail of submachine-gun fire – shot through a lung. Though he was wounded himself Jose Sabate tried to help his stricken comrade, but Lopez's wound was too serious and even with assistance he could not stand up.

'Run Pepe! . . . Save yourself . . . I'm done for!'

Powerless to help his comrade, Jose Sabate escaped amid a hail of bullets. Lopez[3] was taken, unconscious, to the Red Cross Post of Coll Blanc in the Calle del Progreso, together with one of the police drivers who had been wounded slightly in the cross fire.

Lopez was operated on immediately, and afterwards, taken to the Military Hospital where he received further surgery and then, still in a serious condition, taken to the Police Headquarters for interrogation. It was there that he had the satisfaction of learning that Jose Sabate had managed to escape.

It is impossible to try to say why the police decided to raid the house in Torrasa. Jose and Francisco Sabate, together with Penedo, were leaving for France the following day. Francisco wanted to spend the night in the mountains as did Penedo, but Jose preferred to sleep in a comfortable bed and Penedo allowed himself to be talked into doing the same at the last minute. The raid appears, therefore, to have been quite accidental – no one, apart from the comrades themselves and the couple whose flat they were sleeping in, knew they were in that house.

Jose Sabate knew the district like the back of his hand and, although seriously wounded, managed to shake off his pursuers. With a great fortitude he made his way a good distance from the scene of the gun-fight to a tile factory. There he came across a pair of night patrolmen chatting to the nightwatch-man of the factory. Menacing them with his pistol, now empty of bullets, he forced them to hand over a jacket and a pair of trousers. The sudden appearance of an almost naked man, covered in blood and waving a gun took the three men aback. Without protest they handed him the clothes he wanted – something which, one might say in passing, was to cause them a lot of trouble later on when confronted with the *Brigada Politico Social.*

Jose tore up the shirt, and with the help of one of the street patrolmen made a provisional bandage to stop the flow of blood. He then headed for the Rio Llobregat and, mustering all his strength, managed to swim across the river. Finally he took refuge in the house of a comrade some eight miles from the scene of the gunfight, where he knew he would be given shelter.

As Jose struggled for his life, Francisco searched frantically everywhere for him, ignoring the ever present danger to him-self. *El Quico* worshipped his brother, who not only had great courage but was also a man of great intellectual capacity,

92

which Francisco admired. The two men always had a perfect understanding, their ideas being almost identical – not only in politics, but also with regard to action. After forty-eight hours of anguish, *El Quico* finally located the place where his brother was hiding.

The house of Manuela Valerio Ramos in Torrasa was searched meticulously, and the good woman herself subjected to a high-intensity interrogation. The police discovered in her house a list of libertarian prisoners and their families prepared by Francisco Ballester Orovitg during his stay in the Model Prison and later handed over to Jose Sabate.

Jose's escape and the death of a policeman, caused a tremendous fury among the high-ranking officers at the Via Layetana. They had to produce results – and soon – to justify their continued existence. On closer examination of the list found in the house they discovered that one of the prisoners had recently been released from prison on conditional liberty. With their murderous mentality they decided to seek revenge for the death of the policeman on this comrade – who had nothing whatsoever to do with this affair. At dawn on 11 March, 1949 the uniformed assassins knocked on the door of No. 4 Calle de la Torre, in the San Gervasio district of Barcelona. When they identified the person who answered the door as the man recently released from prison they shot him dead at point-blank range, in front of his wife and children. The murdered man, Miguel Barba Moncayo[4] was an old militant known in the Resistance movement under the pseudonym of '*Reyes*'. He was a well-known and popular figure in the Gracia suburb of Barcelona, although he actually lived in San Gervasio.

For her part, Manuela Valerio was obliged to state that the men had been introduced to her through a neighbour from the nearby area of Hospitalet de Llobregat, the suburb adjoining

Torrasa. The police raided this neighbour's address and discovered a large quantity of arms, ammunition·and parcels of anti-Franco propaganda.

Jose's wound needed immediate attention by a competent surgeon. Francisco had treated him with his field kit but this was not enough, so he went to a clinic to find a doctor who had been recommended to him. He told the duty sister the name of the man he wished to see, telling her it was of the utmost urgency.

'I'm afraid if you don't have an appointment he can't see you,' she said.

'I know that is usually the case – but in this case it doesn't matter,' insisted Francisco. 'Tell him I was sent by Dr X (he gave the name of another doctor known to him) and that it is very important that I see him.'

Sabate was immediately shown in.

'What do you want?'

'One of the Resistance has been badly wounded by the police. Get together what you need and come with me,' said *El Quico* forcefully.

'I don't really have any objection to going with you,' replied the doctor, 'but on behalf of the wounded man I must point out that you are not being very prudent, and it could have fatal consequences. I am a surgeon, certainly, but I specialize in hernia and appendix operations. For anything else I'm more or less useless.'

Sabate was somewhat put out by this reply, but the doctor's honesty convinced him.

'Very good, forget I ever came to see you. That would be the best for everyone – including yourself. I'm sorry for the trouble I've caused you.'

Francisco remembered that Pedro Adrover Font (*El Yayo* –

94

'the Grandfather') knew an anti-Fascist doctor, a humanitarian first and last, who never refused his services to anyone in need. After a fruitless search for *El Yayo*, *El Quico* managed to obtain the doctor's address from another comrade.

Once again the doctor gave his services to the cause of Spanish anti-fascism. He accompanied Sabate to his brother's hiding place and treated him successfully. The diagnosis was correct : the bullet had gone right through his body without touching any vital organs. If there were no complications, and fortunately the wound did not seem to be infected, Jose would recover quickly. After dressing the wound, the doctor returned to Barcelona.

Although the most pressing problem had now been solved, there still remained the question of security, as the place where Jose was hiding could not be used for any lengthy period of time. *El Quico* decided to transfer his brother to a new hiding place where he could recuperate in peace and quiet. To facilitate the transfer, *El Quico* approached a peasant he was friendly with and asked him for the use of his cart.

'I must have it. Take whatever its worth. If I lose it you can buy another and if anyone asks you about its disappearance you can tell them it was stolen.' He handed the peasant 40,000 pesetas.

With Jose comfortably bedded down in this vehicle, Francisco made for San Boy, where they left the horse and cart. Disguising himself to look as though he had just come from the local lunatic asylum – to avoid comment on the critical appearance of his brother – they then took a taxi for Martorell. Here Francisco felt he was safe and, with nothing to fear, could obtain everything he required but . . .

Scarcely had the brothers made themselves comfortable in their new hiding place when they discovered, quite by chance, that the police had set watch on an adjoining house in Martorell, where they hoped that at least one of the Sabate brothers would sooner or later appear. The two men found there was a large net thrown around them, and it seemed that every effort had been made to ensure their capture or death.

The house invaded by the police contained a family with two children. One was a girl of ten, and the other a little baby which cried the whole time. Naturally enough the police were on edge with the job they had been given and this was aggravated even more by the constant screaming of the child. At last, one policeman's patience was exhausted and he said to the mother :

'I've had enough of this ! Shut that bastard up !'

'Easier said than done,' said the mother. 'It's time for its feed and there isn't a drop of milk in the house, let me go for some or at least let me send my daughter.'

The police did not want anyone to leave the house as they knew the news of their presence would spread like wildfire and the trap would be exposed. However, with the hungry cries of the child going on constantly they could stand it no longer, so they allowed the mother to send her young daughter – accompanied by a plain-clothes policeman – for milk. Either because he was ashamed of his role, or because he sought to avoid the suspicion which would be aroused if he were seen escorting the child, he let the little girl go into the dairy on her own, while he remained outside the door.

'Guess what . . . our house is full of policemen !'

This remark was enough. It spread around the village and within a short time reached Francisco's ears. He was concerned about this new turn. It would appear that someone had given the address of that house to the police, and it could well be that, by following leads, they would ultimately come to their hiding place. Jose had lost a lot of blood and was still very weak. Now the police were on his trail again. What could he do? He had to prepare a careful escape from the immediate danger. There could be no question of a frontal attack.

Sabate collected all the compromising material in the house and put it in a sack. Disguised as a peasant, he left the house with the sack over his shoulder and set out for Barcelona. There he met some comrades and together they worked out a plan of action. They decided that the best strategy was to play one section of the police off against the other and take advantage of the resultant confusion to effect Jose's escape. In Martorell there was an old militant who had adapted himself to the new régime like the Vicar of Bray and had become a local municipal figure. He was one of those people who always took care to remain in everyone's good books. One of the comrades paid this man a visit, and, in the course of conversation, mentioned to him that the house of 'so and so' was full of police.

'What's all that about then?' enquired the comrade from Barcelona.

'This is incredible and I certainly have heard nothing about it. I'll pop along to the barracks just now to see what they have to say about it,' replied the old man.

Up at the barracks, the Guardia Civil were incensed at this incursion into their territory. It reflected on their status. The effrontery of this outside police group coming into their village and setting up an operation without so much as a by-your-leave.

The ex-militant and neo-Falangist, puffed up with his own importance and accompanied by two Guardia Civil, called on the house occupied by the Barcelona police. The whole affair was beautifully stage-managed. There followed a stormy scene in which prerogatives were invoked, territorial limits discussed and mutual accusations made of abuse of authority and

97

ursurpation of privilege. While the argument raged in the house, *El Quico* – aided by Francisco Martinez (*Paco*) and Santiago Amir Gruanas (*El Sheriff*) and one other, carried Jose from the nearby hideout into a waiting car and whisked him off to Abrera. There Jose managed to recuperate sufficiently to return to France with *Catala*, the guide, and another of the local libertarians from Manresa. He arrived in Toulouse at the end of April, and for a time took on the job of Secretary of the Regional Committee of his home district in Llobregat.

Once the group had passed Jose Sabate safely across the border they returned to Barcelona, with the exception of the comrade whose name has not been mentioned. This young man returned to Manresa after arranging to meet *El Quico* in the Calle Tallers, near the Plaza de la Univerisdad at a future date. On the day of the rendezvous, *El Quico* took his normal precaution of driving past the arranged spot, where he saw a heavy concentration of police. There seemed little doubt that his comrade had been arrested and that the henchmen of Polo and Quintela knew about the proposed meeting.

The young man[5] had, in fact, been arrested on the stairway of the Metropolitan Railway in the Plaza Catalonia on his arrival in the capital. The police were relentless in their efforts to lay hands on Sabate.

In May 1949 another action group crossed the frontier heading for Barcelona. They were all experienced guerrilla fighters: Jose Lluis Facerias (*Face*), Guillermo Ganuza Navarro, J. Marti and Juan Serrano, an ex-boxer known as *El Chofer*. The departure of the group from French territory did not escape the vigilance of the well-organized intelligence service of the Francoist authorities. An ambush was prepared for them near San Lorenzo Savall, just outside Barcelona, on the main road to San Feliu de Codinas. Ganuza and Juan Serrano were the first to cross the road, being the advance party, the others remained some distance behind. No sooner were they both openly exposed when a hail of Guardia Civil bullets brought them down. Ganuza was killed immediately and Serrano was wounded in the leg. Facerias and Marti, hidden in the ditch, opened fire on the Guardia and, under cover of an exploding grenade which Facerias threw in the direction of the ambushers they managed to drag Serrano[6] to safety and escape. Ganuza's dead body remained on the road to San Feliu de Codinas.[7] The three comrades made their way to Barcelona without further incident where they established contact with the other action groups – Sabate, Pedro Adrover, Francisco Martinez and others.

At this period the United Nations were discussing the position of Spain, and a number of South American countries – Bolivia, Peru, Brazil and Columbia – proposed, with the approval of the Political Commission, that the agreement of December 1946 – that no member country should accredit representatives to Madrid – should be annulled. The agreement itself was quite worthless. From the very moment of signing the document it was ignored by all the countries who found it in the least inconvenient. Indeed, Argentina, which did not previously have an ambassador in Madrid, opened diplomatic relations with Spain immediately following the UN Assembly decision against it. When the recommendation to reopen relations was turned down in 1947, other countries went ahead nominating ministers to Franco's Spain and even when the 'Allied Powers' had no official representatives they had trade delegations there, which amounted to the same thing.

However, as it seemed that the exiles were taking the UN Assembly resolutions seriously the Libertarian Resistance decided to organize a series of protests which they hoped would have some repercussions abroad, certainly they could not be as ineffective as the remonstrations in the UN debate.

Some comrades decided that the best thing to do, to cause the maximum sensation, was to have a few well-placed bombs in, for instance, the Bolivian, Peruvian and Brazilian consulates. To do this they split into two groups : Facerias, Adrover and a third comrade to plant the bomb in the Consulate-General of Bolivia, No. 148 Calle Gerona; *El Quico, Paco* and another to take care of the Peruvian Consulate at No. 273 Calle Montaner, and the Brazilian Consulate at No. 88 Ramblas de Catalonia. The bombings took place on 15 May. There was a set-back in the Brazilian Consulate where, on capturing and disarming the guard a pistol went off, accidentally triggering an alarm bell. It was nearly midnight when this happened so Sabate ignored the timing device, set to give them sufficient time to escape, and replaced it with a short fuse which would go off in a few seconds before help could arrive and the bomb be dismantled, or innocent people injured. However, it failed to explode because in his haste to escape, Sabate failed to ignite the fuse properly, and the Brazilian Consul, Noveras Portes, was saved from a nasty shock the following morning.

The other two bombs, however, went off without a hitch. The one in the Bolivian Consulate was placed in the main doorway, the one in the Peruvian Consulate Sabate managed to get on the balcony with the aid of a fishing rod. Both went off together at one in the morning. The two representatives of the Governments friendly to Franco – Jose Maria Puigcerver (Bolivia) and Octavio Cabero de San Miguel (Peru) only suffered the shock of being awakend in the early hours of the morning. The buildings suffered somewhat more, but were not completely destroyed. The aim had been achieved. They wanted an explosive demonstration, and that it certainly had been.

The General of Generals himself, Generalissimo Franco,

arrived in Barcelona on 30 May, but the precautions taken by the security services can be imagined. It was impossible to get anywhere near him. Determined, at least, that the Caudillo should hear a noise if nothing else, Pedro Adrover (*El Yayo*) attempted to place an explosive charge in the *Banco Espanol de Credito* in the Plaza de Catalonia, but was spotted by a patrol and had to make his escape with the bomb in his hand, primed to go off at any moment! He eventually left it under a seat in the gardens of the Plaza, and the neighbourhood was awakened by the blast of an enormous explosion early that morning.

On 3 April another of his bombs exploded in the cloisters of Barcelona Cathedral, causing enormous panic, but no injuries.

These activities, which, incidentally, were denounced by the Communist Party as 'fascist provocation', caused the downfall of the Barcelona Police Commissioner, Manuel Chinchilla, who was succeeded in turn by Jose Albert Rodriguez.

Meanwhile, as the urban guerrillas fought on in Barcelona, the Libertarian Movement lost one of its most dedicated fighters, Francisco Denis, better known as *Catala*. He crossed the Franco-Spanish border for the last time on 29 May, 1949. On his way to Manresa on a mission for the organization, he was arrested near Gironella, but managed to swallow a cyanide capsule carried for just such a situation and died on 3 June – a day of mourning for all resistance groups.[8]

In early June 1949, Francisco Sabate returned to France to spend a few days with his family in their cottage, *Mas Casenove Loubette*, near the Franco-Spanish frontier.

However, *El Quico*, as we have seen, had been sentenced in his absence to a term of imprisonment and the French authorities had no intention of forgetting the matter. On Saturday, 4 June, the gendarmerie arrived in force at the cottage. As Leonor opened the front door to them Sabate fled to the attic –

access to which was gained by a staircase inside the house. This attic also served as a granary. As Leonor argued with the gendarmes in the front-room, Sabate made his escape through a trap door which led back to the hallway, where only a few seconds before the gendarmes had been standing, and slipped out across the fields. However, this was no ordinary routine check. Knowing *El Quico* was in the house, they had taken every precaution to prevent their quarry's escape. The house was surrounded, and as Sabate ran out across the fields the gendarmes let fly a few warning shots, and set their dogs in hot pursuit. Within a short time the dogs had him pinned to the ground with his legs in the vice-like grip of their jaws.

Before the French court, *El Quico* put up a vigorous defence. This hearing took place on 28 June, and he received a two-month prison sentence, but the Appeal Tribunal in Montpelier increased this to one of six months plus five years prohibited residence in the area. *El Quico* was then taken to Montpelier Prison where – as we shall see; he was to spend a year. As a result of this prison sentence the Sabate family was obliged to leave the *Mas Casenove Loubette* and Leonor and the children moved to Toulouse.[9]

The crime, illegal possession of arms and explosives, was Sabate's first offence in French territory and the result of the trial was given great publicity in the Spanish press.

How did he come to spend so long in prison? Earlier we mentioned a robbery by unknown men at the Rhône Poulenc factory in Peage de Roussillon in May 1948. Sabate was accused of complicity in this robbery and the Spanish authorities did their best to complicate matters for him.

Carlos Vidal, the owner of the car used in the attempted robbery in Lyons, was arrested in Barcelona. He made a statement under interrogation to the Spanish police that the car registered in his name, in fact belonged to Francisco Sabate

Llopart, and on 3 May he had been asked by Sabate to drive the car to Perpignan, which he did, and when later asked to take it to Lyons, had refused. It was this statement which prolonged Sabate's stay in Montpelier jail. In the meantime the French police discovered that *El Quico* had sent a telegram to his wife on 19 April, 1948 – less than a month before the attack – from the Post Office at Saint-Fonts which indicated that at least he had been in the area about that time. Among the objects found at the scene of the crime were three berets which were sent for forensic analysis to the police laboratory. Hairs found in the material were alleged by the police chemists to match closely Sabate's, and in all probability the berets had been worn by him.

The car salesman in Toulon, who had sold the car, formally identified Sabate as the man accompanying Vidal at the time of the sale. He also stated that it had been *El Quico* who paid the deposit. However, on 26 July, 1950, the case was thrown out of court for lack of evidence. Sabate hoped that with this acquittal the French police would make no further demands upon him, but this was not to be. The case of the Rhône Poulenc robbery attempt was to follow him until his death – and perhaps it could be said to be the direct cause of his downfall.

---

[1] Toma Gil Llamas, member of the *Brigada de Investigacion Criminal* (CID) for seven years from 1946 to 1953, says in his book *La Ley Contra el Crimen* (Imprenta Pulcra, Barcelona, 1956) 'the car carrying the unfortunate Falangists was identical to the one used by the Commissioner and the resultant confusion led to their deaths'.

[2] The police were quite justified in taking this warning seriously. The signal to the Revolutionary insurrection in Barcelona on 8 January, 1933 was to have been the blowing-up of this very same police headquarters in the Via Layetana and the Civil Government buildings in

the Plaza del Palacio. Anarchist groups placed large dynamite charges in the sewers under each building. The bomb under the Civil Government building did not go off, but the one under the police headquarters did. The only reason it did not blow the building apart was because it had been prepared before-hand and the very size of the bomb did not allow it to be placed near enough to the foundations, where the force would have been at its greatest. See the book by Ricardo Sanz *El Sindicalismo y la Politica – 'Los Solidarios y Nosotros'* (published by author, Golfech 82 – France 1966.)

[3] Jose Lopez Penedo, from Paredes de Cuidad in Orense was born on 13 July, 1915. He was brought before a Council of War on 16 November, 1949 where he received the sentence of death, carried out in Barcelona on 4 February, 1950. He was executed alongside Carlos Vidal Pasanau who had been sentenced for his part in the *attentat* in the Calle de Marina.

I have here some lines from the last letter he wrote to his wife – a few hours before he faced the firing squad:

Dearest wife,

These last few hours of my life that I have left I dedicate to thinking of you and our wonderful daughters. Today will see the culmination of the fears which must have been apparent in all my letters.

It pains me to undo all those illusions which lately you have built up – of my returning to live happily with you and the children.

I repeat what I said in my first letters to you – try to keep close to my parents and the rest of the family.

In particular fond regards to your brother and his family, also to the nephews and their mother. To my mother I would ask you to give her a warm embrace for me and to you and our dearly beloved children I send the last embrace my heart can send you,

> kisses, kisses, kisses, and my last farewell,
> Pepe.

[4] Barba was fifty years old. Sentenced to death after the victory of Franco, he was later commuted and left prison after spending seven years inside. In August 1947 he was re-arrested together with some younger comrades. He had just returned home from prison on this occasion when he was murdered by the police.

[5] He was sentenced to death on 16 December, 1949 but later this sentence was commuted to one of thirty years imprisonment. Many comrades in the action groups, including Francisco Sabate, suspected that he was the man who, as 'Jose Francisco', later wrote a book denouncing his ex-comrades, *Habla mi Conciencia* (ALAS, Barcelona 1956).

[6] Serrano was murdered in a street in Barcelona on 5 November, 1949.

[7] Ganuza had remained in Spain at the end of the Civil War. Imprisoned several times, he was eventually released in August 1948 when he joined Facerias and crossed with him into France.

[8] Born in Leon, *Catala* had been Commissar of the 2nd Battalion of the 121st Mixed Brigade during the Civil War. He was an excellent guide who, from 1943 onwards, constantly took part in missions between France and Spain.

[9] I visited the cottage in June 1972 and found it in ruins. The carefully cultivated fields and the house itself are overrun with weeds. It has been empty since the Sabate family's departure. (Author's note.)

CHAPTER IX

Extermination

In August 1949 the Anarchist Defence Commission in Exile, together with militants of the action groups, decided to reorganize the infrastructure of the groups inside Spain. The reason for this was that many of the groups, such as those of Julio Rodriguez Fernandez (*El Cubano*) and Jose Sabate Llopart, were much too large to maintain proper security. Both groups were split into two. With all the preparations finalized, the action groups began a massive infiltration into Catalonia and, in particular, Barcelona.

The Francoist Intelligence Services were aware of this infiltration and so, suspecting the worst, panicked. They unleashed a holocaust of repression against all the known Anarcho-Syndicalist militants in Catalonia – groups they had previously allowed to exist provided they did not make too much trouble for the authorities. Unfortunately this led to the almost complete extermination of the action groups operating in Catalonia.

On 26 August the group led by Jose Lluis Facerias engaged the Guardia Civil in a gun-battle near the French frontier. Two of his comrades, Celedonio Garcia Casino[1] and Enrique Martinez Marin,[2] were killed in the affray. Another, Antonio Franquesa[3] was badly wounded by a bullet which broke his left arm and punctured his left lung. His life was saved by Facerias and two other comrades who were unharmed.

At the beginning of September a group of well known

comrades led by Ramon Vila Capdevila crossed the frontier into Spain. Among these men was Manuel Sabate Llopart, the youngest of the Sabate brothers. When the Civil War erupted Manuel, the 'Benjamin' of the Sabate family, was only nine years old, and at its tragic end he was still in short trousers. He lived with his parents and had no cares in the world, other than anxiety for his brothers, one in prison, and the other on the run from the police. Manolo was a carefree boy, with a thirst for adventure, who wanted to learn a great deal and travel the world. He left home at sixteen to wander Spain, which he did by jumping trains with his rucksack on his back. He developed a love for bull-fighting and for some months travelled the villages of Andalusia practising passes and thrusts with the young bulls in the meadows. On many occasions he would return home tired and hungry, but within a few days he was off on the road again, without telling anyone where he was going. Manolo travelled Spain from north to south and east to west in search of excitement.

By 1946 he felt the attraction of the life and prestige of his older brother, Francisco, and – without a word to anyone – left for Eus in the Eastern Pyrenees where *El Quico* and his family were living at the time. There he took a job in a local co-operative as a farm labourer. Neither Francisco nor Jose wanted to take their younger brother with them on their risky trips into Spain; indeed, they did their best to persuade him to remain in France to study and learn a trade. Manolo, however, did not want to learn a trade, he wanted adventure – this time as a guerrilla fighter, not a bull-fighter.

He seized his opportunity during Francisco's imprisonment (June 1949) and Jose's absence in Spain to persuade other comrades to allow him to accompany them into Spain. So, during the first days of September 1949, Manuel Sabate, Helios Cihilioli, an Italian anarchist from Venice, and Ramon Vila

107

crossed into Spain. Capdevila was one of the most experienced guides in the organization and on this occasion he was to rendezvous with and accompany the urban guerrilla group of Saturnino Culebras Saiz (*Primo*) to the outskirts of Barcelona. This group consisted of Saturnino, his brother Gregorio, a French comrade, Manuel, Jose C.G., and Miguel A.A. Juan Busquets Verges accompanied them to join Jose Sabate's group, now established in Barcelona. The nine men arrived safely at the outskirts of the small Catalan town of Manresa and without incident. It was here that the first misfortune befell the group. Being extremely tired after their long and arduous journey, they decided to commandeer a car to carry them to their destination. They prepared an ambush on the main road from Rocafort to El Pont de Vilamura. When the first car appeared three of them took up positions in the middle of the road and signalled to the driver to stop – with their sub-machine-guns. The driver of the car made as if to stop but, when he was within a few feet of the group he put his foot down hard on the accelerator and made off at top speed – fortunately without injury to the three comrades. The men reacted immediately and opened fire on the fast-disappearing car, puncturing the two rear tyres and forcing it to swerve into the ditch.

When they reached the car they discovered that a bullet had wounded one of the occupants – a young servant girl about twenty-three years old. The driver was her employer, an industrialist from Manresa. The young girl needed immediate medical attention so the comrades lifted the car out of the ditch and placed it carefully in the middle of the road, telling the industrialist to drive carefully to the nearest first aid post, a few kilometres further up the road. When the police later announced this incident to the press they said that the guerrilla group had killed a young woman. This was a fabrication – the young girl was fully recovered and out of hospital a fortnight later.

Ramon knew that it would only be a matter of hours before the whole area was swarming with Guardia Civil. Hurriedly they buried the more dispensable arms, explosives and heavier equipment and moved off rapidly before the police arrived. They reached the outskirts of Manresa early the following morning where they spent the day hiding and resting in a ravine, safe from inquisitive eyes and patrols of Guardia Civil.

Towards evening it was decided that Saturnino Culebras and Juan Busquets would go to Barcelona to arrange the safe houses for the group's later arrival. On the journey Saturnino and Juan came to a small village where they made their first mistake, one which could have cost them dear. They asked one of the villagers to direct them to the railway station. There was no railway station in the village and this, together with the appearance of the two strangers, made the man suspicious. After giving them wrong directions and sending the two comrades off an a wild-goose-chase, the villager hurried off to inform the local Guardia Civil commander of the presence of the two strangers. Saturnino and Busquets soon realized that they had been misled and were retracing their steps when they saw a lorry load of Guardia Civil approaching them. The lorry screeched to a halt, and as the Guardia tumbled out the two comrades opened fire with their pistols. The Guardia threw themselves to the ground and, as it was by now quite dark, gave the two men the opportunity to make their escape into the mountains before their pursuers realized what had happened.

Early the next morning Busquets walked into nearby Torrasa to buy food and a pair of shoes, his own were in tatters and he had borrowed Saturnino's. He returned to the mountains with the necessary provisions where they had a quick breakfast and then both made their way into Torrasa, where they caught a train to Barcelona.

Once in the capital they made contact with Jose Sabate and other comrades, who informed them that they had prepared accommodation at safe addresses for those comrades still in the mountains. This problem resolved, Saturnino returned to meet the others and bring them into Barcelona. For some reason, however, they hid all their machine-guns in a wood before leaving for the city.[4]

Ramon Vila, Helios Cihilioli and Manuel Sabate accompanied them to the outskirts of the city then, saying farewell to their comrades, headed in the direction of Berga – Ramon's usual theatre of operations. Unfortunately, the earlier incident with the car had caused the mobilization of larger numbers of police and Guardia than expected – the three comrades walked straight into an ambush. Helios died almost immediately in the gun-battle which followed, but Ramon and Manolo managed to escape without injury. Two days later Ramon left Manolo hidden in a little wood while he went to a nearby cottage for food, but this time exceptional measures had been taken to capture Ramon and his accomplice. Patrols of Guardia Civil were strategically placed at all points where the anarchists could take refuge. As Ramon approached the farm he noticed some suspicious movements and turned to escape, to be followed by a hail of bullets – all of which missed their target. Ramon only managed to survive by jumping into a deep ravine, where he almost broke his neck.

Manolo was now alone in strange territory. Shivering from the cold, almost starving, he finally hid his gun and made his way to the nearby road, where he was arrested immediately by a patrol of Guardia Civil. He was taken to the local barracks and there identified as one of the 'infamous' Sabate brothers.

Manuel Sabate Llopart was executed, together with Saturnino Culebras Saiz (arrested in October 1949) at the notorious Campo de la Bota in Barcelona on 24 February, 1950. The Francoist authorities revenged themselves on Manolo for all the trouble and ridicule his brothers Jose and Francisco had brought on them.

At the beginning of October, also near the frontier, while they were resting within a few hundred yards of the border line, the Guardia Civil ambushed and killed Cecilio Galdos Garcia,[5] a well known militant of the mountain area and ex-Commandant of the 126th Battalion (CNT [known as the *Columna Libertad* prior to militarization]) and a member of the clandestine Peninsular Committee of the FAI; Carlos Cuevas, a resistance fighter, and Oltra, a militant from Valencia.

In Barcelona the repression was triggered off by the arrest of a young libertarian and a member of the Talion group, Jaime A., in the Chinese Quarter (Barrio Chino) of the city, while attempting to sell an unusual gold watch to a police informer. The inspector who effected the arrest knew he was dealing with a 'terrorist' when the young man, on being asked to produce his identity papers, showed him a Falangist membership card, withdrawn from circulation shortly before as a result of the discovery of numerous forgeries emanating from Toulouse. Without arousing Jaime's suspicions as to the real reason for his arrest, the inspector waited for the most propitious moment, lulling the arrested man into thinking it was a purely routine and formal matter, before overpowering him by surprise and discovering, when he searched the manacled youth, a Colt pistol and two hand-grenades. Jaime was taken to the *Jefatura de Policia* under heavy guard, thus starting off the chain-reaction of arrests and murders of comrades in the streets, in their own houses and in the police stations of Catalonia.[6]

In Barcelona, on 14 October, officers of the Brigada Politico

Social, effecting numerous arrests, located the young Aragonese libertarian, Luciano Alpuente, known as Madurga, shooting him dead as he stood talking to a friend in the street. Three days later, on the 17th, the police discovered an arms dump near the Llobregat river on the road to Prat and set up a watch on the dump. An action group which came to replenish its supply of guns and ammunition had to fight its way out in a furious battle with the police. They managed to make their escape with the help of hand-grenades, suffering only one casualty, who received a slight wound in the leg. The police, somehow, were receiving good information. They also knew that on the same day – the 17th – at seven-thirty in the evening, Jose Sabate had arranged a rendezvous with comrades in the Calle Trafalgar in Barcelona.[7] It was the perfect opportunity to do away with one of the most tenacious and outstanding members of the resistance. To this end they set up a huge trap covering the whole length of the street as far as the Arco del Triunfo. The time for his arrival passed and they were beginning to think that their information was false. Unluckily this was not the case. At seven-fifty Jose was at a tram stop in the Calle Bruch, adjoining the Calle Trafalgar, when he spotted the police and they spotted him. Opening fire with his pistol, Jose took advantage of their surprise and ran off down the Calle Trafalgar.

Jose knew enough about police methods to realize that this was no chance encounter. He knew he had fallen into a carefully prepared trap, and was therefore on the lookout for any suspicious movements. At the end of the street, in an alley that led to the passage of San Benito and the Salon Victor Pradera, he found that two policemen had been posted there, Miguel Moran Astigarra[8] and Luis Garcia Dagas.[9] Jose again fired first and Garcia Dagas fell with a bullet in his head. Other plain-clothes policemen opened fire, seriously wounding Jose.

Even so, he kept firing and managed to wound another two policemen. Their bravado waned rapidly when they saw how often his bullets found their targets.

Jose, his means of retreat blocked, ran through the passage of San Benito and managed to cross the Plaza de San Pedro where a passer-by helped him into a nearby pharmacy. The chemist, on seeing the wounded man, made him sit down, but Jose, with all his strength now gone, fell unconscious to the floor. In this condition the chemist did not dare treat him and someone ran out to inform the police. At that moment two Guardia Civil officers were passing and discovering the wounded man, ordered an ambulance for him. They told the ambulance driver to take Jose Sabate to the Municipal Dispensary in the Calle Sepulveda, but when they placed him on the stretcher he was dead.[10]

It was a day of rejoicing for the Falangists, a day of anguish for the Resistance. However, the tragic list of murders had only just begun. On Friday, 21 October the forces of repression struck down Julio Rodriguez Fernandez, *El Cubano*[11] one of the organizers of the Talion Group in the Calle Diagonal. A private car, full of police, pulled up beside him in the street and mowed him down in a hail of gunfire, before he had a chance to know what had happened. The same day the professional murderers were at work in the Pueblo Seco area and, using the same methods, took the lives of another two anarchists, Victor Espallargas[12] and Jose Luis Barrao, known as Pepe.[13] Both were unarmed.

The toll of deaths that day did not end there for, at nine in the evening, Francisco Martinez (*Paco*) was killed in the same way. He was shot down at the corner of the Calle Dos de Mayo in front of the very 'Dam' Brewery where he had played as a child. He was twenty-seven years old.

In addition to these street murders, a large number of arrests

113

were made. On 5 November, Jose Perez Pedrero (*Traga-panes*)[14] was arrested on a tram, and the same day Pedro Adrover Font, (*El Yayo*) fell into the hands of the police while on his way home. In the same place, a little later, they shot down and killed another comrade, Juan (*El Chofer*), and later discovered in his house a large quantity of badly needed arms and explosives. The police rounded the day off with the arrest of Jorge Pons Argiles, together with another comrade, and also three Barcelona doctors accused of having given medical assistance on various occasions to wounded members of the Resistance.

The repression was not confined to Barcelona. Apart from operating in the industrial area, the Libertarian Resistance also had many groups in the mountains and forest of Catalonia. Among the places they preferred to operate in were Alto and Bajo Llobregat, where Ramon Vila Capdevila (*Caraquemada*) and Marcelino Massana Vencell (*Pancho*) were two of the best known guerrillas. Another comrade captured was Jose Puertas, a forty-seven-year-old militant from Granada who worked in the mines of Figols. Puertas was savagely beaten-up and tortured in a desperate effort to obtain information, but he replied bravely:

'Only one member of the Resistance operates here . . . that one is me!'

Jose Puertas had played a great part in the Civil War. At the defeat of the Republican Army he was unable to cross the frontier and was subsequently arrested. The brutal treatment he received in captivity seriously affected his lungs. Eventually, when released on provisional liberty, he returned to his home town of Berga where he quickly contacted his comrades in the mountain groups. Most of these fighters he knew as old friends and, in the winter of 1944, he joined them in the mountains and shared their rough life. However, due to his chest complaint, he was better suited to urban guerrilla activities so he returned to the city, where he was of inestimable assistance to the mobile urban groups. He was the contact between Barcelona and the mountains. If necessary, he would go out in all weather, risking everything, and walk miles to warn the guerrillas that actions were being planned against them. The authorities were never aware of the activities and missions he undertook and he was arrested simply because of his previous record as a libertarian activist.

On Monday, 14 November, 1949 the Guardia Civil drove Puertas bound and gagged, together with another two Anarchist comrades, Jose Bartovilo and Juan Vilella – who had also been tortured in the Civil Guard barracks in Berga – to a deserted area and murdered them in cold blood.

Following this triple murder, the Guardia Civil of Sallent went to the house of Miguel Guito and shot him in his own doorway without the least explanation. His only crime was that of being the uncle of one of the most famous of the local guerrillas, Marcelino Massana.

In January 1950 the police wiped out the 'Los Maños' group. Wenceslao Gimenez Orive was taken by surprise and mowed down by gunfire. Although badly wounded, he had sufficient strength and presence of mind to swallow a cyanide capsule hidden in his fountain pen. He was twenty-eight years old.

On the same day another two members of his group were arrested, Placido Ortiz and Simon Gracia Fleringan. Both were sentenced to death and were executed by firing squad in Barcelona on 24 November, 1950.

In the course of this chapter the name of Ramon Vila Capdevila has been mentioned on a number of occasions therefore it seems only proper to sketch in outline a few details of the life of this untiring libertarian resistance fighter as we have no further occasion to refer to him in the story of Sabate. His story merits a book in itself, and it is to be hoped that some day someone will attempt such a work.

Ramon was born in Peguera, near Berga, on 2 April, 1908. As a result of an accident when he was fifteen he was nick-named 'Burnt-face' (*Caraquemada*), but among his friends he was known as 'Wild Boar' (*Jabala*) because of his preference for solitude, independent character and physical strength. Both mother and son had been in the country when a thunderstorm broke and they sought shelter under a nearby tree. The mother was struck by lightning, which killed her outright, but Ramon was only struck a glancing blow causing the above-mentioned burns about the face.

He was of Herculean build, a veritable man of the moun-tains who did not tire easily. This physical strength sometimes led to trouble with his other comrades in the mountain guer-rilla groups, who did not share his ability to continue for days on end with the minimum of food and water and continue to give the impression that he was out for an afternoon stroll in the park.

Ramon joined the Anarcho-Syndicalist National Confedera-tion of Labour at an early age, and, took part in the abortive revolutionary insurrection in Figols during 1932. As a result of this rising Ramon spent the next couple of years in the dungeons of Manresa Prison. The Republican Government did not look kindly on Anarcho-Syndicalists and when Ramon was eventually released, he was forced to move from town to town because of constant harassment by the Spanish Special Branch. On 18 April, 1936, as he was walking with his cousin through the streets of the village of Castellon de la Plana, he was ordered to stop by two police officers. These two agents of 'Law and Order' attempted to apply the *ley de fuga*, but it proved fatal in the case of one of them. After a short gun-battle

116

Ernesto Garcia Bayona, one of the policemen, had a bullet in his head and another in his heart. This man had taken part in General Sanjurjo's ill-fated military uprising in Seville four years previously and, after being punished by the Government with a four-month suspension from duty, was transferred to Castellon police station. The other policeman, Ramon Beas Jimenez, was operated on, but his wounds could not have been all that serious as, after the Fascist victory in 1939, he re-appeared on the scene with the rank of Chief Superintendent.

Caraquemada's cousin, Ramon Rives, was killed in the gun-battle and it was discovered during the autopsy that he had sixteen intestinal perforations from the bullets. *Caraquemada* himself escaped and took refuge in an orange grove adjoining a Guardia Civil Barracks and then, with all his ammunition gone, surrendered to the Guardia rather than let himself be taken prisoner by the Special Branch. He was released from prison on 18 July, 1936 as a result of the policy of opening all the prisons in an attempt to quash the military Fascist uprising.

Ramon played an active part in the fighting in Catalonia during those early days of the Civil War until the Fascist opposition was wiped out, and later was nominated by his workmates as Supplies Delegate of the *Central Termica* (a large factory) in Figols-Las-Minas. Later in the war he became a Commandant in the Carabinero Corps.

After the defeat of the organized working class and the Republican Army, Ramon escaped to France where he was interned (as were thousands of others) in the concentration camp of Argèles-sur-Mer, but managed to escape in 1940 and returned to Spain, where he began to organize the first of the guerrilla groups to continue the struggle against the Franco régime. Unfortunately, however, he was re-arrested while returning to France on a mission a few months later by a German patrol and was imprisoned in Perpignan Gaol for a short time. The Nazi war machine, however, was crying out for labour and so Ramon soon found himself working for the TODT organization in a bauxite mine near Herault. In February 1944 he joined the French Resistance, where he soon became indispensable because of his knowledge of explosives and experience in sabotage operations. After the liberation of France in 1945 he turned, once again, to the struggle against fascism in Spain. It would be impossible to recount all his activities in the Iberian Peninsula from 1945 until 1963 (the year of his death), but the last act of sabotage he was responsible for was the blowing up of electricity pylons near Rajadell in Manresa (Catalonia) on 2 August, 1963.

Many years before, the Francoist police had attempted to implicate him in the murder of the wife of a British doctor holidaying in Spain, Mrs Bernard Joseph Peck, near Puerto de Tosas in October 1951. According to the doctor's statement his car was stopped by two men in blue overalls carrying submachine-guns who ordered both him and his wife out of the car. The doctor drove off, but the men opened fire, shattering the rear window of the car and killing his wife. Later the doctor thought he recognized Ramon as one of his assailants from photographs shown to him by the police. This event took place at a time when the French authorities and press were in the process of unleashing an intensive defamatory campaign against the Spanish Libertarian Movement in exile (as we shall see in the following chapter) and when Ramon returned to France it was not the most propitious moment for him to present himself before a French court in order to prove his innocence. Ramon did not have much faith in bourgeois justice and he most certainly was not the type of man who would allow himself to be imprisoned voluntarily – no matter for how short a period. He was horrified to discover on his return to

France that he had been named by the Spanish police as one of the murderers of the British woman. Following this incident he became progressively a more and more solitary figure as the years went by, but never once did he think of abandoning the guerrilla struggle against Spanish fascism.

On 7 August, 1963, a Guardia Civil corporal and two privates on duty at one a.m. near the castle of Balsarenz, not far from Manresa, saw a shadowy figure make his way towards the Castle through the trees. They called on him to stop but were answered by a pistol shot. The man who died early that morning with a bullet through his heart was Ramon Vila Capdevila. His body was taken to the mortuary in Castellnou de Bages, where it was formally identified by his sister Josefa, who lived in nearby Berga.

The Spanish police needed little excuse to issue victorious press communiqués, eagerly published by the Fascist press, in the same way they had crowed over the deaths of Jose Lluis Facerias, Jose Sabate and others:

'*El Caraquemada*, the bandit, has been killed by the Guardia Civil after twenty-seven years dedicated to crime and plunder.'

The last of the mountain guerrillas had fallen, but by that time other comrades had taken up and were developing the struggle against fascism, not only in Spain but throughout the rest of the world. *Caraquemada* did not die in vain and the new libertarian activists owe a great deal to his inspiration and example.

In France the CNT remained silent as they had done before with Facerias and others. Not once did they rise to their feet to explain to the world who the dead man was and what he had fought for. The Spanish dictatorship took his life, but it was the Spanish Libertarian Movement which dug his grave.

[1] *Celes* – as he was known to his friends, was born in Barcelona on the 25 December, 1922.

[2] *El Quique* was born in Barcelona on 27 April, 1927.

[3] Antonio Franquesa Funoll (*El Toni*), was born in Vich in 1920. He was killed in another gunfight with the Guardia Civil on 19 April, 1950. He was a militant of the Partido Obrero de Unificaccion Marxista (POUM) and an experienced guide who, for feelings of affinity, preferred to work with the libertarian groups. The POUM, the Workers' Marxist Unity Party, was founded in 1935 with the union of the Workers and Peasants Bloc, and the Communist Left. It was described by the Communist Party as Trotskyist though later disowned by Trotsky. George Orwell fought in its column during the Civil War (see *Homage to Catalonia*).

[4] These arms were never seen again. A few days later Saturnino and Busquets returned to collect them, without success. When Saturnino's group was arrested in October they were still without arms.

[5] Cecilio Galdos was born in Santander in December 1902.

[6] See *Franco's Prisoner* by Miguel Garcia.

[7] Three days before on 14 October, Jose Sabate and another comrade robbed the wages van of a construction company – getting away with 734,000 pesetas.

[8] Born February 1906, joined the police in November 1934.

[9] Born May 1917, joined the police in July 1941. A veteran Falangist, he had been sentenced to death by a Republican tribunal. His sentence was commuted. After the war he joined the police corps, and in the course of a few years went through all the different departments: Governmental police, mobile brigade and the Brigadà Politico Social. He was especially notorious for his hatred of political detainees.

[10] Jose Sabate had a wife in France, Emilia, and on his death left a young child.

[11] Julio was born in Havana (Cuba) in July 1918. He was Commander of the 39th Mixed Brigade of the XVIth Army Corps during the Civil War.

[12] Espallargas was a veteran Barcelona militant who worked with the action groups but on principle never carried a gun.

[13] Barrao was severely ill with an intestinal infection when he was killed.

[14] Jose Perez Pedrero was shot by a firing squad on 14 March 1952 in the Campo del la Bota in Barcelona, together with Pedro Adrover Font, Santiago Amir Gruanas (*El Sheriff*), Gines Urrea Pina, and Jorge Pons Argiles.

120

CHAPTER X

Complications

We should mention here another incident which happened in France, and which added to the many complications of Francisco Sabate's life. A Post Office van was leaving Lyons sorting Office in the Rue Duguesclin on the evening of Thursday, 18 January 1951 with a driver and two guards, when a black car blocked its way and three men carrying submachine-guns ordered the driver out of his cab. The robbers were surprised to see two guards come at them from the rear of the van – this had not been foreseen in their plans and after hesitating for a second or so, ran off in the direction of their car, but as they made their escape they gave themselves covering fire with their machine-guns. The whole thing lasted only a few seconds, and the robbers were able to make their escape without any interference.

The victims they left behind in their haste to escape were Arnaud, one of the guards, who was killed immediately, and Louis Morin, the other guard, who was seriously wounded and died on 3 February. Another nine people who were either in the street at the time or inside the Post Office were also wounded and one of these, a sixty-four year old woman, Agust Jard, died as a result of her injuries a few days later on 26 January. The car used in the robbery was discovered a few days later at the bottom of the Jonage canal, near the Croix Luizet bridge in Lyons.

On 28 January the Lyons police organized a massive manhunt

in the suburbs of the city, employing over 2,000 men, including detachments of the CRS. The operation started at six-thirty in the morning and took over twenty-four hours to complete. It involved the questioning of more than 50,000 people within a radius of twenty kilometres of the area of Lyons, and the searching of more than 10,000 houses – without any success. On 30 January a thirty-seven year old Spaniard, Juan S., was arrested and charged with complicity in the affair. Later the names of two other suspects were announced to the Press; Francisco and Jose Bailo Mata, thirty-one and twenty-seven years of age respectively, both Spaniards.

The French Press dedicated whole editions to the story of the 'Spanish Gang' and the Francoist authorities and press, never ones to miss an opportunity, followed up with an intensive defamatory campaign against the anarchist movement in general and the Spanish Libertarian Movement in particular. This hate campaign inciting the French authorities to act against the Spanish movement in exile had a certain amount of success in the beginning. A result of it was the harassment of many comrades and, for some, internment.

The Secretary-General of the Spanish Libertarian Movement in France, Jose Peirats Valls, was arrested in Toulouse on 3 February and the right-wing Parisian daily newspaper *Le Figaro* announced the following day that the 'Spanish Gang' were thought to have been part of an anarchist organization.

When a corrupt or dishonest policeman, judge, priest, army officer, or politician is exposed (something which is becoming every day more common), the integrity of the organization or institution to which they belong is never questioned – at least by the media. A general, for example, employed by a foreign power never serves as an example whereby the army itself is to be condemned. A priest who murders or molests little children is considered to be 'a bad apple', as are policemen who plant detonators and 'verbal' a suspect or person they want to put in prison. Never is it suggested that the institutions themselves are corrupt and dishonest!

However, when the villain of the piece is a member of the organized working class, the capitalist press takes great pains to place the blame for whatever act the person or persons are accused of at the feet of the collective organization to which they belong. This is what happened to the MLE in France as a result of the frustrated Post Office robbery in Lyons. The robbers were anarchists and this was sufficient excuse to mount a vicious hate campaign against the CNT in France. Fortunately, this campaign did not last long, as the libertarian emigrés were not only the most numerically important of the Spanish emigration, but generally speaking their activities and conduct were beyond reproach. A typical example of harassment against the CNT was the arrest of Marcelino Massana (Pancho) in Toulouse on 6 February 1951. The Spanish Government demanded his extradition for alleged 'crimes' in Spain. The hearing took place in Garonne the following month, where the request was refused by the French court and Pancho was set at liberty.

A few words in passing about Pancho. He was born in Berga in 1919. At the end of the Civil War he held the rank of captain, and like thousands of others, was stranded in the port of Alicante waiting for a ship to take him to safety in France. He was arrested and taken with others to the notorious concentration camp of Albatera, built by the Republic to hold 800 prisoners, but which, under Franco, housed at the time 18,000. After a few months he was transferred to Barcelona and there, after serving three years in the Fascist prison, was released on provisional liberty in 1942. Shortly after his release he was informed that he was being conscripted for the army and would be posted to Algeçiras. Massana had no intention of serving Franco, and took to the mountains, where he began his career as a guerrilla.

As with most of his colleagues, to gain a knowledge of the geography of the mountains he spent some time as a smuggler between Spain and Andorra, and later between Andorra and France. After this he dedicated himself exclusively to the struggle against Franco. A few months before the extradition hearing previously referred to, Massana had only just managed to escape from the clutches of the French carabineros who tried to arrest him while crossing the frontier, and as a result of this the French press began a witch-hunt against him. Later he presented himself voluntarily at the court of Saint Girons to answer the accusations being made against him and was given provisional liberty. Massana's description and photograph was posted on every public building in Manresa and throughout the villages in the area of Alto Llobregat. A substantial reward was offered for information leading to his arrest. Needless to say, this reward was never paid out but the photograph which appeared on the Spanish poster came from the archives of the French police, who have shown themselves only too eager to co-operate with their fascist colleagues in Interpol.

We return now to the incident in Lyons involving *El Quico*. One of the arrested Spaniards, Francisco Bailo Mata, made a statement to the police stating that he had been told by a third person that a man called Sabate had been involved in the attempted robbery of the Rhône Poulenc factory in May 1948, and so once again, the police turned their attention to Sabate.

On 2 February *El Quico* was in Dijon, the area in which he had been officially confined, when he was arrested once more and take to the Rue Vauban police station in Lyons where he was subjected to intensive questioning. On this occasion the police acted without any arrest warrant and without first taking their victim before a magistrate. He was held in custody in Lyons for some days without being allowed to see a lawyer. During these 'interviews' Sabate signed what was supposed to be a confession that he had cut the telephone wires in the frustrated robbery at Rhône Poulenc. We can imagine what form the 'interviews' took when a man of Sabate's calibre attempted to commit suicide by throwing himself out of the windows of police headquarters.[1] His only injuries were cuts on his throat and neck from the broken window-pane.

Sabate remained in the custody of the French police for four days before he appeared before the examining magistrate in Lyons, Le Gueut, who ordered preventive detention charging him with, among other things, 'associating with evil-doers'. With this new information the prosecutor fiscal from the Department of Vienne asked the examining judge on the 23rd to re-open the case against Sabate and the others – the charge being culpable homicide and attempted robbery with violence. The defence lawyers wrote to the Appeal Tribunal of Lyons informing it that there had been a number of violations of Judges' Rules – far too many to reproduce here, but including the following:

It can be proved beyond doubt that not only did O......, P......... and Sabate inform the examining magistrate of Vienne that their alleged statements were only signatures which had been obtained by force, but also, something which cannot be ignored, that before the presiding judge Grenoble, in another case other accused who benefited by a stay in execution Pedro M........., P........., Francisco P........., and the same P........., gave similar information regarding the conduct of the Lyons Police, in particular those from the Rue Vauban Station at the beginning of February 1951.

'It should also be pointed out,' the defence lawyers went on, 'that one of the defendants' lawyers, Pierre Levy, who visited Sabate in the St Paul de Lyons Prison on 10 February, 1951, could see clearly the marks on the defendant from the beating he had received at the hands of the police, and informed the President of the College of Advocates, who, in turn, passed the information to the Lyons Procurator.'

The lawyers concluded by saying, 'furthermore, the "confessions" taken on 3 and 5 February, 1951 from Sabate by the examining magistrate, can neither be considered as valid nor regular, as the methods by which they were obtained must surely indicate that they should be struck from the deposition.'

The Instructing Judge from Lyons ordered that Sabate be set free on 13 November, 1952. However, even this decision did not prove to be final, as we shall see later in our narrative.

The nature of the Resistance Movement changed somewhat in Spain at the beginning of 1951. The clandestine work of the different anti-fascist organizations through the years had helped build up the general feeling of discontent which simmered constantly below the surface. Street demonstrations were becoming more and more effective.

In Barcelona in particular, popular feeling exploded in a completely spontaneous way during the protest demonstration against the Tramway Company. It was begun by students, but gradually the whole travelling public and the working class became involved. The tram passengers resorted to an original tactic to express their disgust (the tram company charged much higher fares than for instance, Madrid) – they boycotted the trams. During the second half of February the incidents around this dispute grew in magnitude and, after the 23rd of the month, virtually every tram in the city was being driven

126

away empty of passengers. This gave further impetus to the illegal organizations taking part in the struggle against the régime.

The agitation against the Tramway Company led, on 12 March, to a General Strike in Barcelona. More than 30,000 workers took to the streets to show their opposition not only to the fares increase, but also to the rising cost of living, and above all to the disastrous rule of General Franco. During the course of the Strike many duplicated leaflets were widely distributed and one (which did not in fact emanate from any Libertarian organizations) said:

> *Para arreglar lo de los tranvias*
> *id a buscar a Facerias.*
> *Contra el Requete,*
> *Viva Sabate!*

which translated roughly means:

> To sort it out with the trams
> Facerias is your man.
> To fight against the Requete,
> With Sabate we'll win the day!

The people of Barcelona knew instinctively who were the real defenders of freedom.

The strike spread to Badelona, Torrasa, Sabadel and Manresa and, by 13 March, 150,000 workers were out on the streets. The Government concentrated all its defences in the Catalan capital. More than a 1,000 men of the Policia Armada were rushed by special train from Madrid. Another 2,000 came from Zaragoza and Valencia. The cruiser *Mendez Nuñez* and destroyers *Elcano*, *Gravina* and *Liniers* carrying large forces of marines arrived in Barcelona harbour. The marines reinforced the army and police in patrolling the streets of the city.

Barcelona took on the appearance of a conquered city. People walking about the street were stopped and questioned and within a short time the cells of all the Catalan police stations were crammed with arrested workers. Although the strike could not last long, at least it demonstrated to the régime, which until then had everything more or less its own way, that its claims to have the support of the people were complete lies. This resurgence of mass working-class action forced the dismissal of the Civil Governor, Eduardo Baez Alegria, who was succeeded in turn by General Felipe Acedo Colunga, a man who had distinguished himself by his bitter and cruel persecution of the working class, in the Asturias following the miners' insurrection of October 1934.

---

[1] Whether a suspect who 'falls' from a police station window is driven to suicide by torture, or is thrown out before or after death, varies according to police requirements. It is noticeable that when democratic statesman and scholar Masaryk 'fell' from a window in Prague, Fleet Street poured scorn on Communist Party apologists, using the sick ironic term 'defenestration' to describe the type of apology made then by Stalinists, later echoed when the anarchist railwayman Pinelli 'fell' from a Milan police station window, by Richard Herd of the *Daily Mail* ('he died after falling from a window in Milan') or, more positively dishonest, by Clive Borrell of *The Times* ('he had been found dead after a fall from a window in a block of flats in Milan').

CHAPTER XI

Despair

As a result of these experiences with the French authorities, Sabate lived in the hope that one day an organization could be formed capable of undertaking subversive and guerrilla actions in Spain. To this end he worked for more than six years, but the organization in exile remained split and undecided on this issue, making no concrete attempts whatsoever to fill this organizational vacuum. They were quite content to settle down into passive bureaucratic existence in their new homeland. For *El Quico* a sedentary life was unbearable torture. By the time he had completed his five-year period of area confinement in Dijon his blood was boiling. In the early spring of 1955 some activists of the Spanish Libertarian Movement (MLE), led by *El Quico*, decided to act on their own initiative and responsibility without involving the organization in their activities, but at the same time maintaining a firm hold on their libertarian ideals. They formed the 'Iberian Federation of Anarcho-Syndicalists', whose watch words were 'culture and action'.

It did not take long for problems to arise between Sabate and the organization in exile. *El Quico,* who had no desire to create a split within the organization, renamed the Federation *'Anarcho-Syndicalist Groups'* after discussions with the Secretariat of the Inter-Continental Commission of the CNT/FAI. Even so they were still disowned and attacked by the official organization in exile.

As we know Sabate could not conceive of any other type of action other than that of the battleground itself – Spain. His idea was to make up for the organizational and combative deficiencies in Spain through the 'Grupos Anarco-Sindicalistas'. These groups were organized initially from comrades living in exile and, later, those in Spain. Their purpose was to act as the focal point for the struggle against the Francoist régime.

Sabate's aim was always clearly defined – to act! It never crossed his mind to create his own organization to compete with the parent body. Sabate belonged body and soul to the CNT, and his only desire was to make it an effective tool of the class struggle – returning to it the strength it should never have lost. In spite of all this, when he returned to Spain as delegate from the Anarcho-Syndicalist Groups he did not organize groups in their name, but instead took on the task of forming local federations of the CNT. Naturally, the men he approached were completely in agreement with his ideas regarding action.

Sabate, who would only defend plans and projects which he personally would have been prepared to carry out, arrived in Barcelona on 29 April, 1955 with a group of four comrades. Things had not changed much in Catalonia during his absence. The Governor, Felipe Acedo Colunga, was a boaster, a charlatan, a man intoxicated with his own power and importance, who meted out harsh penalties – even to his own sycophants. Neither had things changed much in police headquarters, apart from the departure of Jose Luis Albert after four years of tyrannical activities. He had been made Governor of Orense and his position in police HQ was taken by Fernando Vives Camino, son of General Vives of the Military Legal Corps, who had, as assessor to General Emilio Mola y Vidal in the Army of the North, during the Civil War, managed to get himself into the Tax Department and subsequently accumulated a large fortune for himself.

Sabate's Group carried with them an abundant supply of arms and propaganda material bestowed on them by friends before their departure. Their bags were mostly full of copies of a four-page publication, *El Combate*, sub-titled, 'The Organ of the Anarcho-Syndicalist Groups'. These copies were part of the first edition of that newspaper, and were dated 1 May, 1955. The main objective was to revive to its rightful position that historic day in the history of the working-class struggle – the First of May. In *El Combate* they recalled the origins of this workers' holiday – the Chicago Martyrs, the history of the CNT and confederal participation in the struggle for workers' rights. The newspaper concluded with a call to the people for three fields of militancy : for the CNT, for direct action against the peoples' oppressors, and for freedom.

Two of the four comrades remained in Tarrasa until Sabate required their assistance. Naturally, after such a long absence, it was essential for him to ensure his contacts were still in existence and willing to participate in his plans. As the group had invested almost all its resources in equipping the expedition to Barcelona and was now almost penniless, it was imperative that funds be obtained quickly. *El Quico* and his friend, after some initial difficulties in renewing contacts in the city, began to distribute their propaganda in the early morning of 30 April. They hi-jacked a taxi and drove through the districts of Sans, Corts, El Born, the Arco del Triunfo and the Carmelo, distributing *El Combate* everywhere they went – neither did they forget to send a few by post to the Jefatura de Policia, the Governor and other authorities in Barcelona.

A rather ingenious method of distribution was later employed by the Group and which did not present quite so much danger to themselves. This was to place dampened bundles of the leaflets on the roofs of parked cars, buses and trams, in such a manner that when the vehicle drove off the bundles would gradually dry and the leaflets blow off in the streets of Barcelona. However, the financial situation rapidly worsened. At one stage, Sabate's plight was such that he did not even have the money to telephone the other two comrades in Tarrasa.

To bring the Group together in Barcelona, Sabate had to get hold of some money. As always *El Quico* thought it best if the operation was supported by a bank – his only source of funds, and which represented the symbol of capitalism and exploitation. However, in order to carry out a robbery, it was first of all necessary to be equipped with some funds and the two comrades did not have two brass farthings between them. On 3 May Sabate and his friend hailed a taxi and drove to the Travesera de Gracia in Barcelona. There *El Quico* told the driver to wait for him for a few minutes. He took the shopping basket he had brought with him and went into a textile shop near the vegetable market. Inside he asked for the manager, and the moment the gentleman appeared he announced those famous words – *'Soy el Quico!'*

Having told the manger who he was dealing with, he explained the reason for his unexpected visit. Without hesitation the manager handed over all he had – or all he said he had – 4,000 pesetas – and Sabate returned happily to the taxi. The first thing he did was to pay the cab driver and then send for the two comrades waiting in Tarrasa to join him, in the city. The four were reunited on 6 May, although the problem of money still remained. However, *El Quico* had a plan.

Later that same day they hired a taxi in the Avenida de Jose Antonio Sicilia. By the time they had reached the *Hospital Clinico* the driver had become slightly suspicious of his passengers. Perhaps he had seen they were armed. He attempted to draw-up at the kerb, saying to his passengers that they should hang on for a few minutes. He had to be convinced at the point of a gun that he should carry on to the address they had given, in the Calle Mallorca. There, at No. 117, at the junction with the Calle Muntaner, was a branch of the *Banco de Vizcaya*. One of the group remained in the taxi, parked a short distance away from the entrance, covering the driver. The other three, one carrying a vegetable basket and all in shirt-sleeves, entered the bank, passing a pair of Policia Armada on guard duty outside the main door. Once inside, the three produced their submachine-guns from the basket and told everyone to remain quiet. One of the group positioned himself in the hallway to keep an eye on the two unsuspecting guards outside, while another kept watch on everyone inside the bank, and the third went with the cashier to the safe. The cashier, frightened out of his life, helped to fill up the sack with 700,000 pesetas from the vaults. This done, they retreated to the doorway and told everyone to lie down, saying they would shoot without mercy the first one to show his face outside the bank. The three comrades then calmly proceeded to make a graceful exit – wishing the guards 'good day' as they passed – and left in the waiting taxi. As they drove off, one of the men from the bank ran out shouting for the police but it was too late – the taxi had disappeared in the traffic. At the junction of the Calle Jose Antonio and the Calle de la Diputacion two of them alighted and hailed another cab. The other two continued as far as the Avenida del Marques de Duero, where they stopped outside the *Cine America*. They paid the twenty-two pesetas on the meter, and Sabate, laughing, then gave the driver a wad of notes as a tip. When the driver arrived at the police station to report the incident, he found to his surprise that the tip came to 7,600 pesetas!

Following this neat job the manager of the textile store received a Giro cheque for 4,000 pesetas, the amount he had 'loaned' Sabate.

To avoid the inevitable police manhunt Sabate and one of the others remained in Barcelona while the other two returned to Tarrasa. The propaganda distributed the day before May Day had alerted the police. The audacious robbery in the Calle Mallorca caused a complete mobilization of all the Barcelona security forces. Chief of Police Pedro Polo called for a large scale search. He ordered the immediate arrest of all the anarchists on whom he had files in the hope of obtaining some clue through what he described as 'interrogation'.

The raids did not produce the slightest lead as to the whereabouts of Sabate or his three friends, but it did lead to the discovery, on 9 May, of the print-shop of *Solidaridad Obrera* and the arrest of seven comrades[1] working there at the time of the raid. These men had no knowledge whatever regarding the activities of *El Quico*'s group. The paper itself had also commemorated May Day – but in an issue produced in the second fortnight of May.

El Quico proceeded with his task of forming other action groups. This work was very dangerous, as the police had all known Anarcho-Syndicalists under observation, and proceeded to arrest them when they considered that their activities threatened the security of the State.

Sabate, as a member of the CNT, was forced to look for support from members of the organization. After having met the Secretary of the Regional Committee of Catalonia *El Quico* arranged another meeting with him the same afternoon to discuss in detail the actions he proposed to undertake and the extent to which they could work together. The meeting place was arranged to take place in the Calle Wad-Ras, in the East End of the city, at three in the afternoon. Invariably Sabate refused to attend meetings in cafés or other indoor places from which it would be difficult to escape in the event of a trap.

Five minutes before the arranged time, *El Quico* drove through the street in a taxi to check the rendezvous, as usual he trusted no one completely. He noticed an over-large number of what appeared to be workers on both sides of the street. This was unusual for that time of day and his suspicions were aroused. He halted the driver a short distance away from the rendezvous and told him to wait. He strolled towards a group who were talking heatedly among themselves. Passing a man in a raincoat, who seemed to be waiting for someone but who started to follow him, Sabate reached the corner of the Calle de Luchana, where he saw a truck full of police. He realized it was a carefully prepared trap.

However, the police in the truck had not seen Sabate's arrival and thought he was merely someone who lived in the street going about his ordinary business. The plain-clothes man following Sabate was signalled by his colleagues to return to his post. The policeman may have thought it strange but, no doubt appreciating that his colleagues knew what they were doing, he returned without protest to his post. Sabate continued strolling for a few yards then turned and retraced his steps. At that moment he saw the Secretary advancing towards him and, without any apparent concern, hailed him cordially. As both men walked to the waiting taxi he informed the Secretary they were surrounded completely by police.

'Impossible,' said the Secretary, 'you must have been followed!'

'Nobody follows me,' said *El Quico*. 'We haven't time to talk about that now, keep walking and don't turn around.' In the taxi they told the driver to drive off and then Sabate, opening his brief-case, produced a Sten gun. With the butt of the Sten he broke the back window – to the consternation of the driver and the Secretary – to be prepared for any eventualities, as the police van was following close behind them. When they

135

reached the Hospital of Santa Cruz y San Pablo, Sabate told the driver to pull up. He was about to advise his companion to make a run for it, but the advice was superfluous. The Secretary already had his hand on the catch and was out of the car and away before Sabate could finish his sentence. The latter could not help smiling. The Secretary of the Regional Committee jumped into another taxi standing nearby and disappeared. Sabate remained there, with his Sten gun at the ready waiting on the police van driving slowly along the road. When it came in range he ran out in the road and opened fire, smashing the windscreen. As the van screched to a halt the driver fell slumped over the wheel and the police jumped out, throwing themselves flat on the ground. The taxi, which had brought Sabate and the Secretary, drove off at high speed, preferring in the circumstances to ignore the fare on the meter! At this particularly crucial moment, *El Quico* discovered he had run out of ammunition magazines. He fired a few shots with his Colt to discourage pursuit, and was off before the police could pluck up the courage to give chase. At the first corner he threw himself against a wall, until he heard the sound of their running footsteps in his direction. Waiting until they were only a short distance away he ran out towards them with the sub-machine-gun on his hip as though he were about to mow them all down. At this unexpected appearance they turned and ran off the way they had come while he gained the necessary minutes to shake them off completely and make good his escape. He ran down a nearby street, stopped a passing car with his pistol and sitting beside the driver, told him to take the first left-hand turn, go round the block, and stop in front of the hospital where there was a taxi-rank. Having changed taxis a number of times he then considered it safe enough to return home.

From this incident Sabate deduced the following: the police

did not know the identity of the man who attended the rendez-vous in the Calle Wad-Ras, since if they had known it was him his reception would have been somewhat different. The police attitude indicated that they intended only to follow, not to arrest, the newcomer and that they were only concerned with widening the net, in order to place the whole organization under surveillance – the intention being to hit with one blow all the Resistance groups in existence or those that might later come into being. Once again, almost incredibly, Sabate had managed to cheat death.

Amongst the various odds and ends which Sabate had collected during his enforced stay in France, was a type of home-made mortar. It was constructed to fire projectiles packed with propaganda over a distance of 200 yards. The charge exploded in mid-air, scattering leaflets over a large area. This novel method of distributing propaganda was tried out during one of Franco's visits to Barcelona, on 28 September, 1955. He hired a taxi with a sun-roof and explained to the driver he was working for the Ministry of Information and was distributing official propaganda to the people of Barcelona in honour of the *Caudillo*. The citizens were extremely surprised when they saw fluttering from the sky thousands of subversive leaflets, printed on fine multi-coloured paper, written in both Catalan and Spanish. This propaganda was signed by Sabate as coming from the 'Libertarian Movement – Committee of Relations'. He did not put the confederal stamp upon it, nor mention any of the Libertarian organizations. For Sabate, the struggle against Franco could not be considered in the light of group or party politics. His only concern was to creat a general climate of insurrection. Victory for him did not consist of building up the power of a political name or tendency, but in the incorporation of all peoples' forces against tyranny.

Sabate was most definitely not an elitist. He knew, better

137

than most, that Franco's régime would only be overthrown through the mass action of the people. However, as a man of experience, who had seen so many mistakes made by the Anarcho-Syndicalists during the Civil War, he knew also that it was even more difficult to maintain victory than to achieve it.

The best safeguard of freedom, Sabate realized, was a strong CNT Trade Union, which was combative, and able not only to make, but to defend the revolution which others, the day after it came, would attempt to destroy. He never forgot the policies and position of the Communist Party during the Civil War which, on the orders of Stalin was dedicated to counter-revolutionary activities and which totally destroyed the revolutionary morale of the people, leading inevitably to defeat. Sabate would sooner have died than have a repetition of this tragic event. It was for this reason he devoted his life to creating groups which would forcibly resist vacillation in the face of this threat. That is why he distributed two different types of propaganda: one the general type of anti-fascist propaganda and the other, as shown in *El Combate*, putting forward concrete and specific anarchist ideas.

Issue No. 2 of *El Combate* came out in July and No. 3 followed in October. They were both two-page productions, and in all the publication ran to four issues. After the downfall of the clandestine paper *Solidaridad Obrera*[2] Sabate produced a special edition, without number or date, in which he said, among other things:

'This is a warning. When they took our "*Soli*" and the CNT members there, they took defenceless men. If they come for us they will find us with guns in our hands and we are perfectly able to defend ourselves against organized violence of the State, using the defensive violence of the organized working class.' It can be seen from this that Sabate refers to the CNT paper as *our* '*Soli*', and throughout his active life he considered anything which affected *his* organization as affecting him personally.

In addition to his 'publishing activity' Sabate also recorded a number of speeches on a tape recorder and, every so often, would arrive unheralded in public places where there were likely to be large groups of workers – factory canteens and so on – and play his tapes. Out of the blue workers at their lunch break would hear speeches no one would have ever imagined possible inside Spain in a public place. *El Quico* was rapidly becoming a legend in Spain. In Catalonia he had been transformed into 'Public Enemy No. 1' of the régime.

He had his critics of course, especially – although it may sound incredible – among the Libertarian organizations in France.[3] There the *Grupos Anarco-Sindicalistas* were denounced as a usurpation, and his activity was severely criticized. He was even accused of being responsible for the police raid on *Solidaridad Obrera.* Accusations of irresponsibility, lack of common sense, and attempting to cause a split in the movement were thrown at him from all quarters.

As an example of these wild accusations we quote from the Agenda and Reports of the VIIth International Congress of Groups held in July 1956. In their report the Inter-Continental Committee of the FAI included a number of paragraphs from an earlier decision taken at a full committee meeting in 1951, stating what type of activities should be carried out in Spain. This was the prelude to a bitter and vicious attack on Sabate and the *Grupos Anarco-Sindicalistas.* The FAI Committee also reproduced in the report a copy of the latest circular distributed by the *Grupos Anarco-Sindicalistas,* following up with the text below:

All comrades active in our Organization know that they have had and continue to have the right to express freely any doubts they may feel, a right nobody has ever tried to restrict. What no one has the right to do in our movement is to divide and split it, creating an Organization within an organization. This is what Georges Fontenis did in the French Anarchist Federation (FAF) with the creation of the OPB.[4] In effect this is precisely what the writers of this circular are asking of the movement.

All groups and militants should realize the gravity of this circular's implications and the responsibilities its authors could have incurred. We should add that this 'self-styled' Federation has published a little paper called *El Combate*, Organ of the Anarcho-Syndicalist Groups. We know for a fact that a close friend and admirer of Fontenis was involved in the preparation of the first issue of this paper – a man who split the FAF and created the *Federation Communiste Libertaire*, which in due course passed bag and baggage over to the Trotskyists.

Finally, another paper, using the name *Ruta*, is styling itself as the Organ of the Spanish Libertarian Communist Federation, a section of the Libertarian Communist International. We do not believe that this paper has anything to do with *El Combate*, unless the Fontenis faction and the OPB are 'fishing in troubled waters' and hope to sow the seeds of disruption and cause confusion by using for their own ends the activities of our irresponsible comrades.

The authors of this calumny signed themselves 'P.T. & C.', and were members of the FAI Committee of Relations. *El Quico* tried in vain to defend himself against these unfounded accusations, and wrote many letters to the organization explaining his position. It was useless. To defend himself properly it would have been necessary to abandon all his clandestine work of resistance in Spain and to have played the sterile and destructive game of circulars and counter-circulars. Deeply wounded, as were so many other comrades at this time, he decided to

140

carry on with what he was doing, and depend solely upon the goodwill of those – and there were many of them – who were willing to help him in the struggle.

The Anarcho-Syndicalist Groups finally ceased activity in the winter of 1956/57 as a result of vicious repression. During this period forty-three militants of the CNT were arrested in different parts of Catalonia, accused of illegal organization and above all of having conspired with Francisco Sabate, against the security of the State.

The organizer and animator of the *Grupos* in France during this period of repression following the discovery of a large arms dump near the Spanish border. He was sentenced *in absentia* on 28 May, 1957 to twelve months imprisonment against which he appealed. The appeal was heard and he was granted a retrial on 12 November at which hearing he was sentenced to eight months imprisonment and five years confinement. He was released in July 1958.

Jose (Lluis) Facerias had been living illegally in Italy since February 1952 but throughout his stay there he had kept in close touch with his comrades in Spain and France. After corresponding with Sabate, he decided to return to Spain to take up the armed struggle once more. So it came about that Facerias and an Italian comrade crossed the Franco-Italian border in February 1956, where by pre-arranged plan, Sabate was waiting for them with a lorry to take them to a hideout in France. They agreed to meet later on a given date near the Spanish border. Before crossing the Pyrenees again, Facerias wanted to see comrades in Paris, Toulouse and elsewhere, and to see for himself what was going on with the organization in France from which he had been separated for so long. The place they arranged to meet prior to crossing the border was a cottage, *La Graboudeille*, a couple of miles from the frontier. It was owned by a French man, Michel Guisset, who lived there with his wife and children. Sabate had got to know this peasant family over ten years before while working in the area as a mechanic building an aerial cable for a tungsten mine in Costabonne. He knew the area like the back of his hand and it was the ideal spot for a secret border crossing. The *Mas Graboudeille* was situated some four miles from the thermal baths at La Preste. Between the *Mas* and the border, a distance of only a mile or so, there was only one other house, owned by Guisset's brother, and some five hundred yards from the border. Between the *Mas* and the thermal bath there was also only one house, *La Barragane*, which belonged to Guisset's sister. To the north, east and west the land was barren and uninhabited – except for a few shepherds and their flocks – but easy to cross!

The group, composed of Sabate, Facerias, the Italian and Angel M.U., met at *La Graboudeille* and discussed their plans. Sabate, as we have seen, was now operating not only outside the organization but contrary to its decisions. This position made him bitter, and working on the principle that his enemies should know nothing about his activities – and this included his enemies on the Committees of the MLE-CNT in France – he asked Facerias to promise not to let the Toulouse Committee know anything about their proposed journey into Spain, nor indeed to have any contact whatsoever with them. However, Facerias had already met members of the Inter-Continental Secretariat prior to meeting *El Quico* at the *Mas*, and to avoid any argument, preferred not to tell him about it. Both held similar ideas regarding the Committees, but Facerias, who so far had not incurred the wrath of the Committees in exile, felt less bitter towards them, and hoped that one day it would be possible to unite all the working class organizations operating for and in Spain. He had some support for this, although perhaps only verbal, which led him to expect some role in coordinating activities, a role for which he was admirably suited. He therefore tried to avoid a radical breach with the different sections of the organizations.

The group reached Barcelona without mishap, but it did not take Sabate long to discover his friend's 'dishonesty'. In Barcelona a letter was waiting for him in one of the 'dead letter boxes' from a friend in Toulouse. It told him in detail about *Face*'s visit to the Committee HQ, in the Rue Belfort. When *El Quico* read this he lost all confidence in his friend. Sabate was very punctilious in his behaviour towards others and considered this to be a complete betrayal of trust and, after a heated discussion which quickly degenerated into an argument, the men split up – a separation which, unhappily, was to be forever. Both of them regretted the stupid incident. Later when news reached Sabate of Facerias' death he wept as if he had lost another brother.

Facerias now found himself alone in Spain, with the Italian who had accompanied him, possessing only the arms and some money given him by Sabate. After such a long absence and without any really safe contacts there was not much he could do. Having fallen out with Sabate, and knowing he must come across him in Barcelona if he stayed there, he decided, bitterly, to return to Italy, which he did in March. Notwithstanding all his trials and tribulations, Sabate continued with his organization of the Catalan Resistance Movement. He was convinced, at a time when everyone else had given up the dream of foreign intervention, that a rising against Franco was imminent. The money he invested as a result of this belief was fabulous – taken as it was directly from the banks. If some day someone takes on the task of auditing Sabate's financial 'accounts' in Catalonia, the results will be staggering !

These funds, however, all went back into the guerrilla infrastructure and were not touched by him, even for his personal necessities, which were very few. He neither smoked nor drank and the household requirements as well as the money to educate and bring up the children was brought in by Leonor, who earned this by working as a cleaning lady. Needless to say, the amount Leonor earned was still insufficient for the needs of the family, but Sabate would not consider taking any of the proceeds of the robberies for his own needs or those of his family.

The large-scale plans which Sabate prepared could not be financed by his activity alone. Later we shall see the terrible repression which followed in the areas where he carried out his operations, which led hundreds of comrades to the dungeons of Franco's prisons. One of Sabate's constant preoccupations in Spain was the setting up of an effective urban guerrilla infrastructure – building bases, organizing groups and contacts – to ensure that when the day arrived they would be in a sufficiently well-organized position to deliver the final *coup de grâce* to the dictatorship.

An important point should be mentioned about these groups. They never carried out any direct action operations apart from the distribution of propaganda and a general proselytizing campaign in their own areas. Neither did the groups outside contribute one peseta to the support of the action groups. The reason for this was that Sabate knew from long experience that this method of support, reasonable when operating legally, was very much counter-productive when operating in secret, for it only served to give the police clues as to the structure of the organization and allowed them to break it up whenever they felt endangered by its continued existence. This could be, and was, heartbreaking, especially when one considers the amounts of time and labour spent in building up a clandestine resistance organization.

For this reason, then, all the money obtained from expropriations went to finance the clandestine network; propaganda, journeys, arms and explosives, false documentation, prisoners aid, and so on; and for the same reason Sabate and all the other activists were vilified in the Spanish press as 'bandits'. At that time (and even to this day) it was part and parcel of most Governmental policies to hide the existence of revolutionary groups and their activities by presenting them as criminals through the media.

On the other hand, however, neither did the exiled Spanish anarchist press attempt to vindicate expropriation as part of the revolutionary class-struggle and the necessity of this activity to support the urban guerrilla groups in their struggle against the terrorism and banditry of the Franco Government. At that time the revolutionary movement had not benefited from the writings and thoughts of the Brazilian revolutionary Carlos Marighela,[5] who in 1968, wrote in his *Guerrilla Operations and Tactics* the following definition:

'Expropriations are armed operations and a guerrilla tactic carried out to finance, support and advance the movement towards revolution.'

As we have said, Sabate financed the groups' activities with the help of the larger Spanish banks, factories, rich landowners and industrialists, but no matter how much money these operations brought in there was never quite enough for the needs of the groups. Following his break with Facerias, *El Quico* dedicated himself to the job of distributing propaganda for the activist groups in Barcelona and the adjoining towns and villages.

On 21 March, 1956, Sabate was walking through the streets of Barcelona when he realized – with a sixth sense developed through many years of danger – that he was being followed. He stopped several times to check, but there was nothing he could put his finger on. However, he instinctively knew danger lurked nearby, and with his friend, who had been accompanying him, took a complicated route to ensure it was not just

145

someone who happened to be going the same way. Turning a corner, he told his comrade to continue walking while he remained pressed against the wall. It did not take long before he knew he was not being over-paranoid. Sure enough, someone was walking quickly in their direction. The man who had been following them turned the corner, and was confronted with two inquisitive dark-brown eyes and the barrel of an automatic pointed at him from the shadows. Sabate demanded the man's papers, but the threatened man was a veteran police inspector, Jose Gomez de Lazaro y Hernaiz[6] who, after his initial surprise, went for his gun. *El Quico* fired immediately and the inspector fell dead on the Montjuich road, in the borough of Pueblo Seco.

The police knew that Sabate and Facerias were both in Barcelona, but, what they did not know was that the pair had split up on arrival. On the following two days the newspapers carried photographs of both men, who were jointly accused of the inspector's death. The photo of *Face* was of police origin as he had already served a prison sentence in Barcelona in 1946 for illegal possession of arms and illegal propaganda. Sabate's photograph, however, came from another source. The Spanish police never had the opportunity to take his photograph and the only photo-record of him was in France. The solidarity between international police forces was becoming stronger as the years went on.

As usual, Sabate was short of the necessary funds for the work he proposed to undertake. Prior to his entry into Spain with Facerias they had planned a robbery of a branch of the Central Bank in the Calle Fusina. Though his break with Facerias forced him to alter his plans somewhat, he did not change his mind about this. He carried it out with unbelievable audacity and smoothness.

The branch office was near the Borne market place and on

23 May, Sabate and Angel carrying a large shopping basket, hailed a taxi and told the driver to park near the bank. It was pouring with rain and the Policia Armada, who normally patrolled outside the bank, were inside behind the revolving doors, standing in the main hallway close to the cashier's desk.

Once inside, *El Quico* pulled a Thompson submachine-gun from under his raincoat. As he did so, one of the police made to draw his gun but, reacting quickly, Sabate hit him on the arm, forcing to drop it. He then disarmed the other and took their pistols.

The bank was crowded with customers. Sabate lined them all up – customers, cashiers and guards. Angel, his comrade, then went round the tills filling up the enormous basket they had brought for this purpose (in their hurry overlooking a very considerable amount). Then, covering the shopping bag over, Angel retreated to the waiting taxi while *El Quico* covered his exit. Giving Angel sufficient time to reach the taxi he brought out what appeared to be an explosive device with a short fuse, which he lit and placed in the main entrance, telling people to keep as far away from the door as possible and to lie on the ground, as the bomb was due to go off in a few seconds. The customers, guards and bank employees threw themselves to the floor and Sabate made his way unhindered to the taxi whose driver was waiting, blissfully unaware that anything untoward had occurred. The fuse burned its whole length, but the anxiously expected explosion did not take place. When bomb disposal experts took the device to a nearby park to dismantle it, they discovered that the contents consisted of sand and a little note which said, 'Just to show you I am not as bloodthirsty as you make out' and signed, 'The Analphabetic.' 'Bloodthirsty' and 'illiterate' were some of the more common terms given to Sabate in the official press.

Together with Angel M., Sabate returned to France on 26

July, 1956 but, unfortunately, Angel was arrested as he crossed the frontier, separately, and having no documents was taken to Prats-de-Mollo police station. In his possession was discovered a 9-mm Star pistol, and he was charged with possession of this and also illegally crossing the border. The court agreed there were extenuating circumstances and gave him twelve days imprisonment.

Meanwhile the organization in exile had solved none of its internal problems. On the one hand there were the numerous committees and commissions, such as the legally recognized MLE/CNT or the tolerated ones such as the FIJL-FAI. On the other hand there were many comrades who argued unsuccessfully in the various assemblies to separate these 'legal' activities – with their bureaucracies and interminable meetings, conferences and committees – from the illegal but constructive work of resistance organization. However, the apathy of the majority of the members in exile was such that it was the bureaucracy that carried the day. If the bureaucracy had chosen to formulate and carry out any sort of combative policy, they could quite easily have shaken the majority of the membership out of their apathy. However, their poltroonery and vicious denunciation of all those who refused to accept their authority served as an excuse for the continued apathy of the majority. The movement was reduced to such ridiculous abstractions as discussing 'the position of the organization in the event of another World War', rather than take any decisions on the war declared against fascism in 1936.

Sabate returned to Barcelona with two men: Angel M., and Amadeo Ramon Valladar, better known as *El Asturiano*, in November 1956. This was the first time Amadeo had taken part in guerrilla activity in Catalonia, however, he had been active in guerrilla warfare in his native Asturias for many years until he decided to cross into France following the decimation

148

of the Asturian guerrilla groups in 1955, where he came into contact with Sabate. In France he began to yearn for action, and was always expressing his desire to renew the struggle against the Franco régime. Amadeo was accepted into the group and although his personal motives and irresponsibility provoked some minor incidents with Sabate, he was willing to accept that all money obtained by the group would be used for propaganda and organizational activities. Because of this Sabate decided to overlook his short-comings.

As usual they left from the *Mas Graboudeille*. The money they carried with them soon ran out and more was quickly acquired. This time the movement's funds were to be supplied by the construction company *Cubiertas y Tejados* of Barcelona. The offices and wages department of this company were at No. 12 Calle Lincoln. The robbery was planned to involve only three men. To work out the details of the robbery Sabate went on his own to the city, leaving Angel and *El Asturiano* in Tarrasa. Once he had made the preparations he called for the other two to join him in Barcelona, where they met at the beginning of December 1956. The operation was planned for the 22nd – the best day for the biggest wage packets, which would include the Christmas bonuses.

The robbery was carried out with the meticulousness of a commando raid. Angel and *El Asturiano* arrived first to check there had been no last minute changes in routine. *El Quico* arrived at four in the afternoon, the appointed time, in a taxi. He got out a short distance away and went straight to the offices. He was surprised to see that his comrades did not follow him, so he retraced his steps to find out what the trouble was.

'What's up? What the hell are you waiting for?'

'There are too many people inside,' said Angel.

The offices of *Cubiertas y Tejados* had one peculiarity. It was a new building with large windows, the interior easily visible from the street. That day, not counting the employees, there were twenty-four people waiting around in the foyer for one thing or another. Through the main door there was a large vestibule where a flamboyantly-uniformed doorman was on duty.

Hearing his friend's remark, Sabate replied abruptly, 'Come on! Don't worry about that! Let's get inside!' He went off and they followed him. All three men were impeccably dressed. The only thing that distinguished them from the other customers were the Thompson submachine-guns they carried under their raincoats. The doorman asked them politely what they wanted.

'We would like to speak to Señor Guillen,' said Sabate.

'Guillen?'

'Yes, Guillen,' replied Sabate, and at the same time, as though it were the most natural thing in the world and he was chatting to an old friend, he put his hand on the man's shoulder, laughing, as though he had just told a joke, and said in his ear, 'If you want to collect your pension don't make the slightest noise or do anything unusual. Just follow my instructions. *Soy El Quico*! Understand? Come with us to the first floor as if we were customers – and get in front.'

'Please . . . I have a wife and children . . .'

'You just remember it. If you do what I tell you you will see them again. Get moving!' *El Asturiano* remained at the doorman's post without anyone paying him the slightest attention. At the left of the hallway was a staircase which led to the first floor, and the three men walked up the stairs, the doorman leading with Sabate and Angel following close behind. On reaching the first floor they saw a little room with three doors leading off.

'Knock quietly on the right-hand door,' Sabate told the

150

doorman.

The door opened and Sabate pushed the doorman into the room following close behind with his Thompson at the ready, indicating to the five employees to stay where they were.

His tone convinced them. He made them stand against the wall with their feet some distance apart so that they were off-balance, and then asked which one was the cashier. The man came forward, and, as directed by *El Quico*, went to the safe which covered the whole of one wall of the office. On opening the door all to be seen were shelves full of nothing but files but, happily, this part of the safe revolved and on the other side was the money. Sabate covered the office clerks with his gun while Angel filled up a sack with bundles of money. Almost a million pesetas! While the sack was being filled, Sabate explained to the clerks the reason for the robbery. He told them that the money was to be used to help the resistance against Franco's fascist régime. When he had finished emptying the safe he told them to accompany him quietly to the basement, for they were going to visit the main strong room before they left the building. To get to the basement it was necessary to pass through the vestibule on the ground floor once again. To their surprise, however, when they got to the foyer where they had left *El Asturiano* they discovered he had all the employees and customers lined up against the wall with his finger menacingly on the trigger of his submachine-gun.

This unexpected move put a stop to their further plans of visiting the strong room. The alarm could go off at any moment. Sabate quickly took a knife and cut as many telephone wires as he could, but there were too many and they were losing valuable time. On the pavement outside a crowd was gathering to watch the spectacle through the windows, grinning. Presumably they thought they were watching the shooting of a gangster film. Sabate announced to the assembled employees and customers that the first man to put his head outside the door would not live to tell the story of his adventure. Angel ran out first with the sackful of money to the waiting taxi which had brought Sabate. The driver, needless to say, was completely ignorant of what had happened inside the office.

'Start the car,' Angel ordered.

'Eh?' exclaimed the driver, 'I'm waiting for someone else ... I don't know you.'

Angel, without wasting time on explanations, produced the Thompson and said, 'Now do you know me?'

The other two joined him almost immediately and the taxi drove off. The driver, not unreasonably, complained that he'd been treated with very little consideration. Sabate took the opportunity of asking *El Asturiano* what had happened on the ground floor while they were upstairs.

'Some people wanted to leave the building – and I had to bring the gun out to prevent them!'

This was no time to discuss the matter and *El Quico* held his peace, but *El Asturiano*'s jumpiness could have caused a disaster. He had been briefed to let everyone go in and out without hindrance, so that nobody would notice anything was amiss.

When they arrived at the address they had given to the driver the group split up. Sabate advised the driver to go straight to the police in order to avoid being held as an accomplice in the robbery. Later, after changing taxis a number of times, they met again at a pre-arranged rendezvous.

It was easily foreseen that a robbery as audacious as this one, against such a large and powerful company in broad daylight, with so much money involved, and carried out by only three men, would provoke an all-out manhunt by the police. Also, of course, they would be looking for *El Quico*.

Obviously they had to stay hidden for some days without venturing into the streets, and this was how they spent 23 and 24 December. The following day Sabate told his friends he was going on a short journey to a village in the province where he had to attend to some urgent business. After insisting that his friends did not move from where they were, under any pretext, Sabate – disguised as a peasant, made the trip and was on his way back that same afternoon. When he returned, Angel M., had gone. At first he was angry, but as the hours passed and his comrade did not return, he decided to go out and look for him. Taking his usual precautions, he called at several addresses where Angel could possibly have gone, but there was no trace of him. More and more worried, he headed for the house of a widow who lived with her son in the centre of Barcelona, in the Diagonal.

As usual, instead of calling at the front door, he went through the garden and knocked on the back door. The woman's son answered the knock and, when he saw *El Quico*, quietly signalled him to run. Sabate, always quick in his reflexes, immediately jumped to one side. Bullets whistled past his ears. In a moment he crossed the garden and disappeared over the wall. Fortunately for him the police had occupied the house but were waiting in the front-room, supposing that if he did come he would call at the front. How did they know the house? What were they waiting there for? Everything seemed to point to Angel's arrest. Later the mystery was cleared up. The intimate collaboration of the international police forces, to which we have already referred, had enabled them to find through the interception of correspondence between France and Spain, the address of a married couple who lived in the Traversa de Las Corts. Following the robbery of *Cubiertas y Tejados* the police raided this house at two a.m. on 23 December. Subjected to the usual methods of interrogation, the unfortunate tenant of the house, Miguel F., confessed to the police what they already knew from their colleagues in France – that Sabate sometimes used the address as a 'dead letter box'. As it was possible Sabate would call there, the police arrested the couple and took over the flat. For further security, they also occupied the house of the man's mother-in-law – the one in the Diagonal, where Sabate arrived and where he escaped, after being shot at, by pure chance.

The imprudence of Angel M. rang up the curtain on a fresh tragedy. As Sabate guessed, Angel had indeed been arrested. He had gone to the flat in the Traversa de Gracia and walked into the trap prepared for the group by the Brigada Politico Social. It was now certain that the house where *El Asturiano* and Sabate were staying, in the old town, was no longer safe. Neither were any of the other houses known to the arrested man. Sabate had a great deal of confidence in Angel, but knew that soon he would have to talk – interrogation methods in Spain had been perfected throughout the years to a fine art – but he would take his time about it. Sabate and *El Asturiano* had to leave immediately.

They left in the nick of time, at nine in the evening. The police arrived an hour and a half later with something like a small army. They broke into the abandoned flat and, although they found nothing, they knew they were hot on the trail. On the table the evening meal was laid out, but nothing had been touched.

The first thing Sabate had to do was to save all the important material he had collected. This material was kept in another flat he rented in the Calle Bassegoda, in Barcelona's East End. He called on another comrade to help him, and together with *El Asturiano* they took a taxi to the flat where Sabate left his two comrades in the doorway while he ran up the stairs to collect the material – arms, explosives, leaflets, tape recorder, mortar charges and so on. While he was busy packing he heard a warning cry from the street – the police were coming. From long experience he knew that when the police came it was not a question of hiding or hoping they would finish their rounds. Either you ran immediately or you died on the spot.

He was surprised when he ran to the door way and found no sign of police. His two friends explained that the cry had come from the taxi driver who had dropped them and who had just fled with the car. Obviously he had thought there was something suspicious about his passengers – perhaps he had even recognized them. What made matters worse was that they had left a bag containing a large amount of money in the back seat. No doubt the driver would immediately inform the police, as there was a station close at hand. There was now no possibility of the hard-won material being saved.

Two street night patrolmen, who had heard the driver's shout, were passing and saw the three men. One of them, gun in hand, came up and asked what they were doing and for their identity papers. *El Quico* replied, 'I am *El Quico*! Understand? Now get the hell out of here! I don't want to have to kill a poor bastard like you!' The second patrolman came up to find out what was happening, but by this time his colleague had sized up the situation and said, returning his gun to his holster, that everything was in order. The three comrades then got out of the district as fast as they could. First they had to find a safe hiding place, since before long the whole of the Barcelona police force would be on their trail. Where could they be absolutely safe? Angel M., knew too much – too much for comfort, anyway.

When they were a respectable distance from the scene of the incident, Sabate told his friends to wait for him while he checked if they could stay in a nearby house. On his return, much to his surprise (yet another on that day of upheavals) he saw they had both disappeared. Walking up and down, he waited for them to return, spending an hour of absolute anguish. Lurking in the shadows, he saw in the distance patrols of Policia Armada and Guardia Civil and, sensing danger at hand, once more barely managed to escape their clutches. Hailing a taxi, he passed through the network closing in on him. Watching through the windows for possible control points, he suddenly thought he was seeing things. Lo and behold, there on the pavement was *El Asturiano* about to cross the street. They had met by sheer coincidence. Sabate ordered the taxi to halt and beckoned him to get in. According to his friend, while the two had been awaiting Sabate's return the other had gone for cigarettes and did not return. Soon after he noticed some suspicious activity in the area and so decided to move on himself. He was afraid the other had been arrested or maybe even gone to denounce them. *El Quico* could only accept this explanation.

The pair, still in the taxi, headed for a building site in Monte Carmelo, in the north of the city, where earlier they had hidden a bag containing 100,000 pesetas and a submachine-gun. When they got there they found the bag had disappeared. It seemed that Angel M. had broken sooner than expected and they still had to find a safe hideout until the police activity had died down. None of the usual hideouts offered any security whatever. They needed somewhere completely unknown to Angel and they finally came to a desperate conclusion, but the only one open to them. As it was now quite late and the streets rapidly becoming deserted it was obviously dangerous to continue walking around much longer without running the risk of being challenged by the street patrols, apart from the fact that they were exhausted after such a hectic day.

They left the taxi and went into a bar where there were still a few customers lingering on, chatting. When the first of these customers made his farewells, they followed him discreetly to his house, in the Calle de Cartagena, in the north-east of the city. As the man felt in his pockets for his key Sabate went up to him, stuck a gun in his ribs and said, 'I am *El Quico*! I and my friend are coming up with you to your home. I am sorry but we have no option.' The man lived with his wife and twelve-year-old daughter. Sabate courteously explained to them that he would cause them the least possible trouble, but while he and his friend stayed there nobody could leave, although nothing would happen to them if they did not try to do so. However, the man calmly pointed out that this was not a feasible plan. Both he and his wife went to work, and if they were absent for any length of time somebody would almost certainly call round to find out what was wrong. Sabate agreed with him, and after a few minutes' reflection decided that the couple should go to work as usual but they should telephone the school to say that their daughter was ill. The plan had its dangers, but Sabate had no alternative. Everything went off perfectly, and the two were able to stay in the flat for some forty-eight hours. This gave them time to recover their strength and to think of some place which the police could not discover from their interrogations and searches. Sabate and *El Asturiano* then decided to move to another flat in Barcelona. However, on leaving the flat in the Calle Cartagena *El Quico* repaid the family handsomely for their forced hospitality.

Sabate had been up against it many times before, but never as much as now. The Barcelona police were working tirelessly, night and day, to eliminate once and for all Spain's 'Public Enemy No. 1'. To make matters worse, a bomb exploded on the plinth of the Victory Monument in the Plaza de la Victoria, on the morning of 30 December. The bomb did not do much damage to the monument itself, but, being a large explosive charge, it broke.a good many windows in the vicinity. This monument was a favourite target for Resistance explosives – marking as it did the numerous commemorative festivals of the Franco régime and its victory. In the form of an obelisk, it was erected originally to the memory of Francisco Pi y Margall, the apostle of federalism in Spain and a disciple of P. J. Proudhon, considered by many to be the 'father' of the libertarian movement. In 1940 the Fascists pulled down the commemorative plaque together with the bust of the great federalist, and converted it into a symbol of the armed victory of tyranny. The police immediately attributed the explosion to Sabate. So tightly did they draw the net around him and so convinced were the police hierarchy of his imminent arrest that many of the senior police officers spent their nights in the *Jefatura* waiting for the news that *El Quico* had been arrested or killed.

However, Sabate and *El Asturiano*, managed to escape the immediate clutches of their enemies, and remained undercover for more than a month without showing any signs of life. Then, at the beginning of February 1957, Sabate decided to return to France. In the meantime Angel's arrest and the information extracted from him by torture had unleashed a ferocious repression in Catalonia. With the assistance of special brigades sent from Madrid to assist their Catalan colleagues, houses frequented by Sabate and his comrades were raided, and the occupants or owners, who were not directly involved in his activities, arrested. From 31 December, 1956 the tally of police victims taken from their homes was – fourteen in Tarrasa, three in Olesa de Monserrat, three in Esparraguera, eight in Ripoll, six in Moya and ten in Barcelona.[7]

By this time Sabate had lost all confidence in *El Asturiano*. He had come to know him better in adversity and so despised him, recognizing him for what he was – a man without any

158

principles whatever.

The repression and the police activity in the Llobregat area was particularly harsh, and so Sabate decided to take a different route across the Pyrenees, one by which he had not travelled for a long time – through Santa Coloma de Farnes, outside his usual scene of operations. He realized it would be dangerous to embark on such a long journey with so much money – he still had most of the money from the *Cubiertas y Tejados* robbery – with a man he did not trust.

There was a woman in Barcelona at that time – at her own request as she is still alive we shall give her the fictitious name of Maria. Sabate trusted her completely and had worked with her on many occasions in the past. She had just undergone a serious operation, and wanted to return to France – in fact she was already preparing to go when Sabate called on her. He explained his problem, the fears he had concerning *El Asturiano* and the necessity of being accompanied by a third person. Maria pointed out that in her condition she would be more of a hindrance than a help. Sabate promised the journey would be done in short stages, which she could manage, and that she would not have to carry anything. Maria, who really wanted to go with Sabate, was easily convinced.

The date of departure was fixed for 6 February, and they arranged to meet in the district of San Andreu. Sabate arrived dressed as an old Catalan peasant – complete with limp. He wore a beret, a long black scarf and on his arm a basket of fruit. Under the fruit was his loaded submachine-gun and mountaineering equipment. The two of them got into a train compartment, where a little girl stood up on seeing the old man and offered him her seat. He accepted it graciously. *El Asturiano* took a compartment further down the train, with his luggage just like any holidaymaker. In this way they arrived at Granollers, where they waited for two hours for another train to take them on the last stage of their rail journey to the small village of Hostalrich, near Gerona. They avoided the town and headed straight for the mountains, where they prepared for their long walk to the frontier – dressing in thick trousers and heavy climbing boots. It was evening when they set out on their journey and, at daybreak, they stopped in a wood, had a sandwich and went to sleep – the three of them taking it in turns to stand guard. It had been eleven years since Sabate had last travelled this area, consequently he thought this route less likely to be watched than any other.

Every evening they moved forward, walking slowly so as not to tire Maria, and stopping frequently to conserve their energy. During the day they rested, hidden in the woods, and three days went by like this without incident, apart from the fact that Sabate seemed unusually jumpy. The truth of the matter was, however, that he was lost and hadn't the slightest idea where he was. After a couple of days they all realized it when they found themselves at a place they had passed three days before. *El Quico* cursed himself furiously. Not only had they lost three precious days, but their food supply was rapidly diminishing. Now they did not have a slice of bread between them.

To restock with supplies they decided they would have to leave the mountains and get nearer the road. Eventually, in the distance, they saw a charcoal-burner's cabin which they approached with caution. The Guardia Civil often used these cabins for sleep and rest. *El Asturiano* remained outside as Sabate and Maria entered the cottage. In the half-light they saw two people sleeping – a young man about twenty years old, and what appeared to be his grandfather. Sabate woke the young one and in a low voice asked him the road he should take to a certain village. The boy then woke the man who turned out to be his father. The old man sat up, obviously in a bad mood, looking at the strangers. Sabate repeated his request.

'Get out of here,' grumbled the old man. 'I don't know anything and I don't want to know anything!'

However, Sabate patiently repeated his request, this time in Catalan, which seemed to give the old man some confidence in him. The father told them that all the charcoal-burners in the area had been warned the day before of the obligation they had to inform the Guardia Civil of the movement of any strangers in the area. They had also been reminded of the dire penalties involved if they failed to do so. The old man insisted they should go as soon as possible and promised not to say anything, but if they were seen near his house it would cause him a lot of trouble.

The three comrades left, accompanied by the boy who was to direct them on their way. He explained to them that his father had belonged to the Trade Union Movement and because of this had been arrested and tortured by the police. After the war he had spent two years in a concentration camp and since then had refused to involve himself in any type of political activity. After a short while the boy hesitated for a few seconds and then told them to wait while he went back to the cabin. Outside they could hear the shouts of the father and the pleas of the boy, and after a few minutes, he returned with a large loaf of bread and gave them the information they had asked for. It was so explicit that they were able to get well on their way without any further problems. By this time they were well into the mountains and, as the land was so rough and wooded, they decided to travel by day. During the journey they came across many more charcoal-burners who greeted them, but made no attempts to involve them in conversation.

That evening *El Asturiano* complained that he had to drink some water as he was very thirsty. As a result of a stomach operation he was constantly obliged to drink large quantities of water. Sabate, always conciliatory, changed the route. They went down into the valley where they hoped they might find some water and where they could see huts built either for the charcoal-burners or wood-cutters. In the vicinity of one of these huts they discovered three demi-johns which had been left almost buried in the ground to keep the wine fresh. They drank gratefully and filled their flasks. Sabate paid for the wine by leaving some money under one of the demi-johns.

Once again they made their slow way back up the mountain slopes. Maria was so tired that when they finally sat down she immediately fell fast asleep. Soon after, however, her friends had to awaken her. They had heard the sound of shooting nearby. It may have been a poacher, but it was best not to tempt providence and they continued walking as far as they could manage. Sabate knew he had to get out of the area as soon as possible – behind them they had left too clear a trail.

Once again the problem was water. While crossing a little bridge *El Asturiano* said he heard water below and went down to the side of the stream, but there was nothing there except sand and pebbles. The ground was becoming drier and more sandy and covered with brambles and briars which they had to fight their way through with sticks. When they finally came to more open ground their hands were covered with bleeding cuts from the thorns and spines. Maria, much smaller than her two companions, was pitifully scarred on her face. However, by daybreak they came at last to a pleasant green pasture with a flowing brook of fresh water. They drank their fill, restocked their flasks, and, after bathing their scratches, continued on their way. While walking they lost all sense of time and, as they pushed on the land changed again, as if by magic. Suddenly there were rocks and boulders everywhere – the way blocked by huge mountains and not one blade of grass to be

162

seen. They travelled slowly without making much progress and using up a great deal of their energy. Once again on the open mountainside, they were forced to travel by night, and in this rocky terrain there was always the risk of twisting an ankle, or suffering some worse injury. At last, however, they crossed this difficult zone and Sabate set about looking for a place where they could rest for a few hours. He managed to get them to climb up the craggy slope of a mountain to reach a plateau where they thought they could rest away from the sight of prying eyes. There, exhausted, they slept like babies.

Maria was the first to awake at daybreak, and when she looked around had to hold back a cry of horror. The little plateau where they had spent the night ended in a sudden precipice and, a short distance away, clearly visible, was a secondary road running past the entrance to a large farmhouse. She woke her comrades quickly to tell them where they were, and they all laughed merrily, seeing they had chosen to spend the night in one of the most dangerous places in the area.

They made their way down the mountainside quickly and took refuge in a wood. They were hungry and their food was gone again. In a field they discovered a lettuce which Sabate and Maria shared between them – El Asturiano refused to touch it. About ten in the morning they came across a little cottage where, at the door, they noticed two little boys playing happily. They went up to them and asked if their parents were in. The children told them that their father was in prison and their mother had left early that morning to go to the village for some shopping. The three comrades decided to wait for the woman of the house to return and hid themselves a short distance away, where they could watch the road that led to the house. When the woman returned Sabate and Maria went to have a word with her while El Asturiano remained hidden in the background. The press had given a full description of the fugitives, but the police had not known of Maria's presence in the group and were alerted for two men, not a man and a woman. In conversation with the woman Sabate was told that her husband was a Socialist and had been arrested by the Guardia Civil following his attendance at a left-wing meeting in the village. For three years he had languished in Gerona Prison. The woman sold them some eggs, a rabbit, bread and wine, for which *El Quico* paid generously – also leaving behind him some money as a gift. The woman wept with gratitude.

Once again they camped in the mountains and, while the men skinned the rabbit and prepared the fire, Maria took advantage of the hot sun to bathe in a nearby stream, then she had a long sleep. When she awoke the banquet was prepared – roast rabbit. Later, contented, they waited for the shadows of evening before continuing their journey. Now the ground was less stony, and they made good time, but the sky soon grew overcast with black clouds and it began to rain. It poured down that night and by daybreak the three were soaked to the skin, until they came upon an abandoned farm. There was plenty of straw in the barn which belonged to a nearby farm, and they made their bed there. It was the first time they had slept under a roof since their departure from Barcelona.

Sabate and *El Asturiano* fell asleep almost immediately, but Maria could not close her eyes as the barn was full of rats, which impudently ran over the bodies of the two sleeping men. She was too frightened even to lie down. When Sabate awoke he examined the nearby farmhouse. It was Sunday and, as far as he could see, the only occupants were two women, one of them quite young. He decided to present himself and his friends as holidaymakers. Sabate had a most enchanting voice when he spoke in Catalan, and had no difficulty in convincing the women to sell them a couple of hens, some ham and wine.

He asked if he could cook them there in the farmhouse and the two women rapidly agreed. As he chatted to the women of the house, *El Asturiano* and Maria plucked the hens. Then, as he was peeling the potatoes, he saw two men coming up the road leading to the farmhouse. Maria suggested that they make a run for it, but the girl came in and told them it was her father and brother. Sabate returned the pot he had removed from the fire, in readiness to take with them in case they had to make a rapid exit, and waited. The women introduced them as holidaymakers who had bought some provisions, but the father informed them abruptly to collect their things immediately, and ordered them out of the house. After some argument between father and daughter, the men eventually gave in, and allowed them to eat the meal they had prepared in peace. During the meal Sabate won the confidence of the father without difficulty. Once on friendly terms, he told them more or less the same as the charcoal-burner – that the Guardia Civil had been to the house warning everyone of the terrible penalties they would incur if they were not informed of the presence of strangers in the district. Sabate told them he and his friends were crossing into France to look for work. Once again the presence of Maria prevented the identification of the travellers with the two men wanted by the Guardia. After some persuasion, Sabate managed to talk the father into sending his daughter to the village to buy some provisions for them – bread, tins of milk, jam and so on.

Finally Sabate told him they needed a good night's sleep and asked if they might spend the night in the stable, to which the man finally agreed. There were no rats in the stable and the three spent a peaceful night.

Early the next morning the daughter appeared, bringing with her a steaming pot of garlic soup. It was pouring with rain outside and, after the meal, Sabate asked if they could remain until it had cleared up. This time, however, the man's mood had changed. He told them to leave immediately, begging them that if by any chance anything happened to them not to say they had stayed at his house. Before they left Maria left an envelope for the daughter of the house on which was written 'For R., to buy a raincoat'. R. was the daughter and inside the envelope was more than enough money to buy her one for every day of the week.

They pushed on that day through the pouring rain, but their spirits had risen considerably. By this time Sabate knew where he was and amused himself by pointing out the landmarks to them. *El Asturiano*, however, got into the habit of falling behind – at one time they lost sight of him altogether. Sabate shouted for him but he took a long time to answer, even though he was not far away. When he eventually caught up with them Sabate said, '*Hombre*! You gave us a fright then!'

El Asturiano gave a malicious grin – no doubt he felt the reason for the fright was the fact that he was carrying all the money from the robbery.

Two days went by without incident, during which they covered a great deal of ground, mostly at night, with everyone in good spirits. Turns at guard duty were scrupulously observed: two slept while one kept watch. The ground was much easier going now; spring was in the air and the going was pleasant. Perky little squirrels watched them as they went by, every now and then a rabbit would jump across their path, the frogs croaked in the ponds, and occasionally the travellers would stop to gather chestnuts to eat.

At dawn on the third day they saw a farmhouse a short distance from where they were camped. Sabate and Maria went to buy provisions while *El Asturiano* remained hidden as before. They returned with eggs, bread and wine only to discover that he had disappeared, having taken with him his rucksack, machine-gun and walking-stick. This time there could be no doubt about it : he had run off. This betrayal, doubly painful because he had already foreseen it in Barcelona, made Sabate lose complete control of his temper, something that rarely happened. He paced backwards and forwards like a man demented, cursing to himself. Finally Maria managed to calm him down. 'But, *hombre*! It's not the end of the world! He's gone with the money – so what? Look on the bright side – he could quite easily have killed us and here we are, still alive – don't jump about so much! He might be watching us at this moment, killing himself laughing.'

Sabate sat on a boulder and looked around him. His eyes rested on a nearby hill. Lowering his head he thought for a moment and then said in a loud voice, 'There's only one thing for us to do now – we shall have to go back to Barcelona.' He stood up and walked towards the hill. Maria followed him without answering. The hill was densely covered with briars and scrub and they had to tear their way through to the top. In spite of the dense vegetation, however, it looked as if the summit would be bare. They moved as quickly as they could, as though they wanted to get out of the area as soon as possible and make straight back to the city. Suddenly Sabate caught Maria by the arm whispering to her to remain quiet. Further up they could hear the sound of footsteps and the breaking of twigs. It was as *El Quico* thought, *El Asturiano* was ahead of them. He was moving forward when Maria grabbed hold of him.

'Don't go. He'll kill you. At the moment he's prepared for anything and you'll be like a sitting duck for his machine-gun from up there.'

He halted. A quarter of an hour later they heard the footsteps returning in the opposite direction. *El Asturiano* had gone to check if they had in reality gone off in the direction of

Barcelona, but it was not easy to see the road from the top of the hill on account of the thickness of the scrub.

Sabate was inconsolable. In a low voice he told Maria that the money was meant for the Resistance Groups, to help the comrades behind bars and their families. When he had unburdened his miseries on Maria, *El Quico* lay face down on the grass for an hour. She did nothing to distract him and at last he decided on a course of action. He spread out his maps and bus timetables, examined them carefully for a few minutes and then told Maria, 'Before six o'clock tonight we've got to get to the nearest village.'

'Which village is that?'

'Santa Coloma de Farnes. We are sure to meet the slimy bastard there. He'll try to get some provisions there and pick up a bus in the village.'

They started off on the road which Sabate reckoned was the one *El Asturiano* would have taken. The ground was sandy and Sabate walked with his eyes fixed firmly on the ground.

'What are you looking for?' asked Maria.

'His boots are the same make as mine. I want to find his tracks.'

As they travelled on a change came over Sabate. He was happy, very happy. The boot marks were visible. *El Asturiano* was astute, but not enough to deceive Sabate. To avoid leaving a trail the fugitive had drawn the branch of a tree behind him. Who but he would have taken such precautions?

They reached a place where the road made a wide curve and where there was a path, evidently used as a short cut by travellers. The trail ended there. Sabate walked down the path a few yards and returned with a branch recently cut from a tree. There was no doubt now, they were hot on the trail of *El Asturiano*. Sabate and Maria continued along the path and soon came on to the Santa Coloma road, but decided to wait until nightfall before entering the town. Maria took advantage of the halt to change from her rough mountain trousers into a skirt. They walked into the village as evening fell.

Sabate tried to work out the possibilities of meeting his un-suspecting erstwhile friend. The village was quite large, but he was convinced that *El Asturiano* was here somewhere since, although he had some hours' start, he was not so stupid as to risk walking into the village in broad daylight. In all prob-ability he had done the same as they, and waited until evening. When the couple reached Santa Coloma the church bells were ringing out the hour of six. As they walked through the market place Sabate saw their quarry. He was in a shop on the right-hand side of the street. He had to be careful as he did not know how the other would react. *El Asturiano* was quite capable of shooting it out in the middle of the town.

The streets was almost deserted so *El Quico* told Maria to hide while he edged closer to the shop. Maria felt as though she were about to faint. Her knees were trembling. The ex-guerrilla came out of the shop – no longer carrying his knap-sack, but a villager's shopping bag – walking quickly and care-lessly. As he passed the doorway, Sabate stepped out – con-fronting him.

'Hello, what happened to you? You had us quite worried for a while . . .'

The other's face was beyond description. He dropped the bag containing the food, and, just at that moment, the shop attendant came running out shouting that he had forgotten his bottles of wine. He stood indecisively, looking first at the woman and then Sabate. The latter told *El Asturiano* to go and collect his wine. When he returned with the bottles, which he gave to Maria, who had by this time joined Sabate, it was obvious he had been drinking heavily. Together the three walked away from the shop with Sabate a little way behind the other two. Once safely outside the village *El Quico* called a halt and demanded an explanation from the other. He explained, in a drunken manner, that while he was waiting for Sabate and Maria's return he had seen four Guardia Civil. He picked up his rucksack and ran off. They had called on him a number of times to stop, but he ran on until he reached the village. He said his feet hurt, and gave other idiotic excuses in the same vein. He went on to say that he knew he would meet them in Santa Coloma – his main worry had been to save the money and divert the Guardia Civil away from the farm where his friends were.

Sabate listened impassively without interrupting then said, 'One thing I don't understand . . . we saw more than four Guardia Civil.'

'Yes, there were at least eight,' affirmed *El Asturiano* enthusiastically.

'And the money – where is it?'

'I've got it hidden just outside the village.'

'Well, let's go and get it. You remember where you put it?'

'Oh, yes. Let's go!'

Maria did not believe that he had hidden the money anywhere and made discreet signs to Sabate to look in the shopping basket, but Sabate did not believe, in the circumstances, that the other was still capable of deceiving him.

For three-quarters of an hour they walked around the outskirts of the village without Sabate losing sight of his companion for a moment. If *El Asturiano* had any hopes of making a run for it he was doomed to disappointment. He knew that an escape now had no chance of success and, finally said to Sabate, as if bemused, 'What are we going around like this for? What are you looking for?'

'The place where you put the money,' Sabate answered coldly.

170

'Ah, that! The money! I've got it with me, in the basket, of course! *Hombre*! Where did you think it was?'

And there it was, well wrapped up in plastic to protect it from the rain. The bag was also well-stocked with ham, sausages, tins of sardines, tuna fish, even chocolate and sweets.

El Asturiano stopped to light a cigarette. As always, in the dark, he took off his jacket and knelt down, his face almost on the ground as he lit the match. Sabate noticed that the only gun he possessed was a pistol, in his shoulder holster, and asked what had happened to the machine-gun. His companion replied that he had thrown it away in order to travel faster. Sabate was about to strike him but managed to control himself, although he was shaking with rage. Smoking his cigarette *El Asturiano*, shrugged his shoulders and gave more explanations, each one more confusing and contradictory than the previous. Sabate and Maria listened in cold silence.

Supper that evening was magnificent – squid, fresh bread, desert, even champagne – *El Asturiano* was sick after so much wine, and the champagne added to the fear he must have felt. Even he could not have been so stupid as to imagine that he had deceived Sabate. The cold manner with which Sabate had accepted his story must have been more alarming than any show of anger. Before starting off again, Sabate called Maria to one side and told her to keep behind *El Asturiano* while he travelled in front. If he made the slightest suspicious move she was to hit him on the head with her heavy mountain stick.

As they crossed a bridge *El Asturiano* leaned on the parapet as though he were about to faint, but with his right hand inside his coat clutching the butt of his pistol. Sabate turned back when he found his companions were remaining behind, but was signalled to by Maria to remain where he was, as their supposedly sick friend had his hand on his gun. Sabate, however, approached his companion with his machine-gun at the ready on his hip, and his finger on the trigger.

'What's up?' he asked.

'He's sick,' replied Maria.

'Let's find a place to rest, then.'

El Asturiano said he felt better and insisted they carry on. Maria, who was watching him carefully, noticed however, that his hand never moved from his shoulder holster as they continued on their way.

As dawn they halted in a wood where they threw themselves down to rest, *El Asturiano* lying facing his fellow travellers. Sabate indicated to Maria that the pistol was pointing straight at them although covered by the jacket. As though he were looking for a more comfortable spot he changed places and sat behind *El Asturiano*, but the latter turned round to face him once again. This arrangement did not suit his plans at all. The game was played several times during the night and Sabate never close his eyes for a minute.

Later in the afternoon, while Sabate was resting at the foot of a tree, *El Asturiano* who appeared to be working something out in his mind, came up close to him, took out a knife, and grunting spasmodically, cut off a branch, stopping the knife a close distance from Sabate's head and at the same time giving Maria an evil grin. As the hours passed the atmosphere grew more tense. Sabate was visibly tired, but dared not go to sleep. Maria suggested to him that he give her the machine-gun and try to get a few hours sleep himself.

Taking advantage of a moment when *El Asturiano* had gone into the bushes, presumably to relieve himself, Sabate and Maria held a brief discussion in a low voice.

'He's going to kill us,' she said.

He agreed.

'I don't like the look of it, he'll stop at nothing to get his hands on that money.'

172

'What shall we do, shouldn't we get away from him before he kills us?'

'I don't know,' pondered Sabate. 'I'll think of something.'

'Well, you had better think quickly,' replied Maria.

Eventually before nightfall, Sabate decided on a course of action. He told Maria to take *El Asturiano*'s gun from him the moment he gave the signal. However, another two days passed in this tense atmosphere of suspicion before the opportunity arose. In the meantime Maria kept a close watch on him and noted where he kept the three knives hidden in his clothes. The girl also kept an eye on Sabate, waiting for the signal, but he ignored her mute pleas and gave no explanation.

At nightfall on the second day, as the group prepared a meal before starting on their nocturnal march, *El Asturiano* made the mistake for which *El Quico* had been waiting. He lifted his flask to drink – with both hands. Normally he only used his left hand, leaving his right one free. Sabate did not waste the opportunity and jumped up pointing his pistol at him, telling him not to move and keep his hands up in the air.

Sabate's sudden move had caught Maria unawares – as it had *El Asturiano* – but she did not take long to react and, approaching him from behind, removed the pistol and the three knives which had caused them so much anxiety. She threw the weapons towards Sabate and continued searching his pockets. *El Asturiano* protested vigorously, demanding to know why he was being treated in such a manner. He grew frightened and fell to his knees, retelling again and again the story of the Guardia Civil. Still on his knees he pleaded with Sabate for his life – apologising abjectly for behaving the way he had. He was convinced his last hour had come. Despite the fact Sabate had been without sleep for several nights he still had the strength to deliver a sermon. He explained to the other what he already knew, that the money was for no one's personal gain and was to be used solely for the struggle against fascism. With words that came from his heart he attempted to try to make the other understand how despicable his conduct had been and exhorted him in the future to behave like a man. He went on to say that the machine-gun he carried would be used in the defence of the three of them, and warned him that he had reached the end of his patience and would not tolerate any fresh tricks.

'Get one thing into your head,' said Sabate. 'I ought to shoot you down like a dog, but I won't. Until I leave you safe and sound in France I'll defend your life with mine. If we have only one slice of bread left, we'll share it with you, but don't forget for one minute, the slightest false move and I'll kill you. If you behave you'll have no complaint to make of me.'

El Asturiano continued to protest on his knees. Sabate who had sat down on a tree trunk, got up ordering the other to do likewise and then, strapping the bag containing the money to Maria, handed her the pistol and kept the knives for himself. The look in *El Asturiano*'s eyes made Maria shudder. However, he made the rest of the journey walking a safe distance between the two of them. With only two stages remaining before they crossed the frontier Sabate was exhausted. His eyes were sunk deep into their sockets, and though free from the fear of a bullet in the back, he was never really sure what treachery the other might be planning. That day, however, *El Asturiano* made a humane gesture. Sabate's state was so pitiful – he was walking along almost in a trance, tripping over the smallest obstacles – that *El Asturiano* threw his stick into a ravine, and said, '*Quico* – please go to sleep, please – even if it's only for a few hours.'

Sabate believed him and lay down on the grassy verge where he slept for four hours. He woke refreshed and in a good humour. When they came to share out the food, he hesitated for a moment – and then passed one of the knives to *El Asturiano*. On the last night of the journey there remained only half a tin of condensed milk, which they reserved for Maria. Sabate pointed out a view visible from the mountain and told his companions that it was the frontier line. It was bitterly cold, but the nearness of the border gave them wings. A short while later they were standing on French territory – all three, forgetting the hardship of the journey and the bitterness between them – holding hands and dancing like children. They had left Barcelona on 6 February and it was now the 19th. They had spent nearly a fortnight in the mountains.

Sabate knew the terrain he was on now like the back of his hand and he gleefully recounted the different adventures he had experienced there – the agricultural collective he had tried to found, the time he had been chased through the mountains by the dogs of the gendarmerie, his arrest.

That day the only thing they had to eat was some mouldy chestnuts Maria discovered in the bottom of the rucksack. By nightfall, *El Asturiano* fell ill. They helped him to a nearby house, where Sabate, in Catalan, asked for shelter from the occupant – a man of about fifty years of age. He felt sorry for them, and told the travellers they were welcome. His wife prepared a meal and beds for them and sat Maria beside a roaring fire. *El Quico* explained to his hosts as they ate, that he was a guide and was bringing his brother and sister over the border to find work in France. The following day Maria went to collect the documents and papers which they always left at a comrade's house in French territory when crossing the border into Spain.

One last detail of the long, hazardous episode proved that *El Asturiano* had plotted his treachery as far back as when he and Sabate planned their journey, and its objectives, to Barce-

175

lona. The man looking after the documents told Maria when she arrived that the ex-guerrilla had not wanted to leave his behind when the group left France.

Before leaving his treacherous companion[8] Sabate handed him 25,000 pesetas and 40,000 francs, telling him he never wanted to see him again. And so it was.

[1] After spending a long period in custody, three of the accused were granted bail. When the trial finally took place in April 1960 they were sentenced *in absentia* having fled in the meantime to France. One of the three was Antonio Miracle Guitart who, we shall see later, lost his life with Sabate in his last battle with the Guardia Civil.

[2] *Solidaridad Obrera* appeared once more, three months later, the 40th issue, and dated the first fortnight in August.

[3] It is not as incredible as it may sound to a Spaniard steeped in the tradition whereby anarchism was an integral part of the labour movement. In democratic countries, and especially those where the existence of a libertarian movement has not necessarily been synonymous with the working-class movement, it has never been possible to form anarchist organizations which remained such (as distinct from anarchist groups within the revolutionary struggle). To form what is, in all but name, a political party means one is unable to express one's revolutionary ideas for fear of suppression of the organization which in turn must of necessity have a reformist programme and disdain any revolutionary activity, which seems a small price to pay for 'legality'. As it grows older, such a movement must become empty, useless, a platform for the 'liberal' or a 'veterans' home for the ex-militant. This happened to the CNT in exile but also, as proved at the Carrara Congress in 1968 (where the translator was the British Delegate), to similar ageing movements which had sunk into social-democracy and become superfluous since there was no lack of much more powerful social-democratic movements, or in the case of 'new left' movements, into liberalism or pacifism, and so to a position indistinguishable from the left of the Liberal Party.

[4] The *Organization Pensée Bataille* was a breakaway organization formed within the French Anarchist Federation to win it over to political activity. Under the leadership of Georges Fontenis, it managed to break away from the FAF and form the Libertarian Communist Federation, gaining control of the Anarchist paper *Le Libertaire*. It collaborated closely with a Libertarian organization in Italy – the GAAP – *Gruppi Anarchici di*

176

Azione Proletaria, led by Pier Carlo Masini. Both organizations claimed to be representative of the Anarchist movement in their respective countries, but had only a brief existence.

5 Carlos Marighela was born in Salvador de Bahia (Brazil) in 1912. The son of a Greek father and an Italian mother, he was a communist until he rebelled against what he called the 'bourgeoisification of the Communist Parties of Latin America'. In 1968 he founded the National Liberation Alliance (ALN), which dedicated itself during its initial stages to robbing banks and collecting arms in order to build up the infrastructure necessary for the first guerrilla groups operating in Brazil. Marighela was killed in an ambush he was lured into by two priests in November 1969 in Sao Paulo.

6 Born 28 June, 1909, Gomez fought on Franco's side in the Civil War, and soon afterwards (1941) joined the Barcelona Police Force.

7 Forty-three people who had been arrested at this time, were tried on 14 July, 1958 by a Council of War. At the time of the trial twenty-seven were on bail after being detained for six months, and others had been in custody. Angel was sentenced to thirty years imprisonment.

8 Amadeo Ramon Vallador, *El Asturiano*, born in Fabero (Leon) on 24 May, 1920, committed suicide in 1963 in Perpignan on being informed by his doctor he had cancer.

CHAPTER XII

Death

Once again *El Quico* had made fools of the entire mobilized police forces of Catalonia. He did not realize, however, what was waiting for him in France on his return. The repression unleashed in Catalonia continued, the more violent because he had escaped – but the long arm of the Spanish police could even reach him across the Pyrenees. As we have seen, Angel's carelessness had brought him to the cellars of Police Head-quarters in the Via Layetana. There he was interrogated day and night in the offices of the Regional Brigade of the Political and Social Investigation Division, by Police Inspectors Cesar Rodrigo Rodriguez[1] and Jesus Martin Garcia.[2] These gentle-men forced him to sign a full confession in which were details of *El Quico*'s activities not only in Spain, but also in France. They had already managed to dismantle a good part of the organization in Catalonia, and now attempted to destroy Sabate across the border.

From a statement extracted from Angel a report was sent to the French authorities who acted immediately. The text of the application for a warrant reads as follows:

To the 'Renseignements Generaux'.
reference: Deposit of Arms in the Eastern Pyrenees.
subject : According to reliable sources of information a cache of arms (machine-guns, pistols, grenades) has been created by a group of Spaniards in the Preste area of the Eastern Pyrenees. It is in the

immediate vicinity of the *Mas Graboudeille*, beneath a pile of stones at the side of a wall; four or five kilometres west of La Preste (Map Ref : R.603/13) E.M. map scale 1 : 50000. The cache consists of Thompson and Sten sub-machine-guns, Colt and Star pistols, offensive grenades, explosives and ammunition.

The farmhouse is occupied by two French Nationals known as Juliette and Michel Guissot. It is highly likely that this arms dump was created by Francisco Sabate, known as the head of the 'specific' groups of the Spanish CNT (apolitical), but better known as one of the Organization's *franctireurs* who generally works on his own initiative. Although denounced by the Spanish CNT in exile, his actions are tolerated for political reasons, and also because of the fear he inspires. His punitive methods are well-known.

We should point out that Sabate has served a number of sentences in France, been expelled and subjected to territorial confinement. He has continued to be the subject of an extensive investigation dossier. The *Mas Graboudeille* is used by him as the departure point for his clandestine activities in Spain. Included in this report are two drawings by our informant showing the exact position and plan of the *Mas*.

At midday on 9 January, 1957 fifteen gendarmes from Prats-de-Mollo and other brigades positioned themselves around the farmhouse. In charge of operations was Gendarme Sub-Officer Boulbes. Michel Guissot, the occupant of the *Mas*, was informed of the reason for the raid, but he emphatically denied the existence of any arms dump. His denials were to no avail, however, and he was placed under arrest. The area was thoroughly searched by gendarmes using mine detectors. A

179

small wall led off from the courtyard of the house and ran for some distance beside a cart track. At one point there was a mass of boulders six foot across and, when the gendarmes removed the stones, they found a hole lined with slate to protect it from the damp. Inside was an empty fifty-litre petrol can placed horizontally, and from it the police collected the following:

1 9-mm Sten submachine-gun
1 Mosch machine pistol
1 box 9-mm bullets
3 kilos mixed ammunition
4 magazines for a Sten gun
4 magazines for a Mosch machine pistol
3 magazines for an automatic pistol

In addition to the above there were holsters, and other equipment, all in perfect condition.

Michel Guissot told the police he was unaware of the existence of the arms dump, but was taken to Ceret where he was subjected to a lengthy interrogation. He was shown a photograph of Angel M., together with the drawings and plans of the *Mas* prepared by Angel, and finally, the confession which went into great detail about Michel, his wife and family. He finally confessed to knowing about the arms and was imprisoned pending trial.

A warrant was issued for the arrest of Francisco Sabate Llopart, charging him with illegal possession of arms and ammunition.

So it was that *El Quico* found himself with all these problems on his return to France. In addition to the warrant for his arrest, there was also the organizational dispute with the MLE/CNT in exile over the founding of the *Grupos Anarco-Sindicalistas*[3] and his own moral and material obligations to the comrades arrested in Catalonia. His activities at this time were summed up in a bulletin issued at the beginning of September by sympathetic militants of the CNT/FAI in exile.[4]

In the last few years, with or without the agreement of members, the Confederal Organization, specifically that in exile, has abandoned the active struggle in Spain. One group of comrades who had been fighting in the Interior for many years in agreement with the decisions of the Organization in exile, decided to carry on the struggle at their own initiative and risk, and for this reason formed the Anarcho-Syndicalist Groups.

It took some time owing to the many problems we faced, but slowly our organization took shape, making contact with those comrades who wanted to give some positive help. In Tarrasa, which has always been well-known for its revolutionary activity, the comrades formed a small group with whom we made contact. They were all veteran militants and well-known in the CNT. These comrades were completely isolated and at no time had any contact whatsoever with the CNT in exile. They approached us for help which we gave readily whenever we were able to do so. With the material we supplied they managed to broaden their field of action to the outlying areas of Tarrasa. At the beginning of 1957 there were a number of arrests in the Tarrasa region. Amongst those arrested were two men and one woman, comrades who previously had been presented as delegates from the Interior to the National Committee in Toulouse. The National Committee at first refused to receive them and, when finally, they did decide to see them it was too late and these comrades had returned to their factories and work-shops.

Owing to our Anarchist and Trade Union activities of propaganda and organization, the police arrested forty-three militants and sympathizers. Our legal aid to them and our moral and material support was to the utmost of our abilities and did not cease for one moment. In spite of all our difficulties, and with the relatively small number of people we could count on, we managed to make contact with the prisoners within three weeks and prepare a list of their names. We handed the list personally to the Inter-Continental Secretary, who had already been informed of the arrest of these comrades. We can prove that seven months after this list was handed over the prisoners had not received the slightest moral or material aid from him. On the contrary, we can prove that the opportunity was taken to sow seeds of doubt and confusion amongst the militants in exile regarding the arrest of these comrades.

Nevertheless, through our efforts we managed to get thirty-eight of these comrades out on bail after seven months captivity, organizing lawyers from France and Madrid to act on their behalf.[5]

Yet some of our so-called comrades attempted to defame our conduct in this matter – calling us robbers, bandits, criminals in exactly the same way as our fascist enemies. They do so to justify themselves to our movement for their cowardice and inactivity.

We continue and shall continue in our struggle inside Spain. We consider that inertia is the death of the revolutionary spirit. We shall ensure the voice of anarchism will be heard in every corner of Spain, and everywhere in Spain too we will show our solidarity with our persecuted and imprisoned brothers and sisters.

We have reproduced part of this letter because it shows quite clearly the relationship between *El Quico*, at a particularly difficult time for him, and the MLE-CNT in exile. However, Sabate was a man of his word and before concerning himself with his own pressing problems he did everything possible to help his arrested comrades in Spain. He sent 300,000 pesetas to help them – nearly all that remained from the *Cubiertas y Tejados* wages robbery.

As a result of the circular issued by the FAI the *Grupos Anarco-Sindicalistas* were disbanded.

El Quico took it for granted that he had to live as an outlaw in Spain, in fact he could not conceive of being there in any other circumstances, but it was less understandable to find himself in the same situation in France. Following his lawyer's advice, he contented himself with appealing against the sentence passed by the court in Ceret. Had he wished to do so, he could have said that the arms dump had nothing to do with him, and, in fact, could have quite easily have produced convincing evidence of this. However, he felt it was his responsibility as a militant to admit the arms were his, and to be used in the struggle against Spanish fascism. The appeal was successful and the case was heard again, this time in his presence, at the Civil Tribunal of Ceret on 12 November, 1957. The tribunal accepted there were mitigating circumstances, but also bore in mind that he had already been sentenced for a similar offence on 6 October, 1949. He was therefore sentenced to eight months imprisonment and five years area confinement. He was taken direct from the court to Perpignan Prison and a few days later transferred to the Penitentiary of Montpelier. The Franco Government took advantage of Sabate's arrest to apply for an extradition order against him, but fortunately this was refused by the French Government.

Sabate was released on 12 May, 1958, but it was a restricted freedom since he was confined to Dijon for the next five years, in accordance with his sentence. He came out of prison depressed by the indifference of his friends in the Organization to his fate. Dejected, he made his way to his place of exile, Dijon.

Jose (Lluis) Facerias returned to France from Italy in February 1957. He wanted to take up the struggle in Spain once again. He had been in contact with the different organizational committees as well as with the isolated comrades to discuss the idea of preparing a coherent plan of action in Spain. As usual, however, in France, his proposals to the Organization fell on deaf ears. Now he could see, at last, what had caused the emnity between the Organization and Sabate. He would dearly have liked to join up with Sabate again, but *El Quico* still felt strongly about the disagreement in 1956 and had avoided all contact with Facerias. It was a great pity the two comrades did not get together, they could have cleared the air of many things, and at least Facerias would have never gone into Spain the way he did.

Facerias' friends had offered to pay his fare to the Argentine, where he would have good friends and solid contacts. However, this was not to be. Spain called him – as it did Sabate – irresistibly.

In making his plans, Facerias showed a certain lack of caution on this occasion. Normally he was a very careful individual, taking no risks, yet now he allowed himself to be seen everywhere without taking any steps to disguise his identity. Everyone knew he was going back to Spain. Together with an Italian comrade, Goliardo Fiaschi and a Spaniard, Luis A.V., he decided to cross the Pyrenees. However, the Fascist authorities must also have known of his presence in France and possibly of his planned journey to Spain. When the group attempted to leave, the crossing proved to be impossible. The Spanish border guards were too numerous and the area they intended to cross saturated with patrols. The three men waited near the border for two days before the opportunity came to cross the line unobserved, even then the risk they took was very great.

184

On Thursday, 30 August Facerias had a rendezvous at the junction of Calles Dr. Urrutia and Pi y Mollist with the Paseo de Verdun, almost directly in front of the main entrance to the hospital of San Andres. Facerias arrived not knowing that his two comrades had been arrested. However, as usual, before the meeting he took a taxi through the area to check that everything seemed normal. By this time the police had, however, learned a lesson from their previous mistakes and changed their methods accordingly. They knew from experience how difficult it was to surprise men like Sabate or Facerias in the street and had therefore mounted an 'invisible' operation.

Not a car, not a policeman in disguise, no suspicious vans parked in the area, absolutely nothing to be seen anywhere. Instead all the houses in the vicinity of the rendezvous had been occupied by policemen, soldiers and Guardia Civil, and all the windows facing onto the street were shielding an enormous number of automatic weapons – waiting. The moment Facerias arrived and was identified the police opened fire on him – the first volley hitting him in the ankle and fracturing his shin bones. Badly injured, he grabbed his Walther P.38 pistol, the gun he always preferred, and against a thousand difficulties, not even knowing where his attackers were, he crawled to the cover of the trench, part of a nearby road works at the corner of the Paseo de Verdun. Sheer instinct of self-preservation gave him the strength necessary to climb over and fall like a stone nearly twelve feet into the excavation in the road. It was a terrific shock, but he retained consciousness and had just taken a hand-grenade from his pocket, to blow himself or his attackers up – it is not known which – when he was ripped apart by a hail of bullets fired by the police, who had by this time surrounded the trench. He died still holding the unprimed hand-grenade.

Although obviously dead, with his blood soaking the ground,

the body was taken to the Hospital Clinico where nine bullets were removed. In his wallet they discovered his entire fortune : 1,000 francs and 500 pesetas, an identity card in the name of Jose Luis Soler, and five magazines for the Walther automatic.

Police headquarters issued an official communiqué to the press evocative of a major war-time operation, announcing that the police action had involved a number of soldiers from the Barcelona Barracks seconded to the Social Brigade (Special Branch) under the direct control of Juan Estevez and the Commissioner, Pedro Polo Borreguero, plus a detachment of the Guardia Civil under the command of General Juan Luque Arenas.[6] Like many other instances of police actions and repression in Spain the death of Facerias had been initiated in France. When Sabate was arrested on 12 November 1957, barely two months after the death of Facerias,[7] the French police – after asking him ironically if Facerias happened to be a friend of his – gave him a surprisingly detailed account of the murder. They told him how, when, where and with whom he had crossed the border, even the precise spot where he had gone over – Lamanère, in the Eastern Pyrenees.

When Sabate left prison in May 1958 he started work for a central-heating firm – Mauvais and Chevassu – in Dijon. Prison had affected him a great deal, but the air of freedom soon revived his spirits. In spite of the vicious slanders directed against him, both through the Fascist press and the Organization, he discovered he could still count on many friends who had remained loyal to him. Slowly he managed to build up his contacts – in Paris, Lyons, Clermont Ferrand – and ignoring the confinement order, he travelled the length and breadth of France, taking part in meetings and consistently putting forward his position in regard to the activist struggle in Spain.

There was no lack of people who thought Sabate unsociable

or elitist. These views always came from people who either knew nothing whatever about him or had reasons of their own for attacking him. It is true that Sabate was forced to act time and again on his own initiative, as he was constantly confronted with demagogues and hypocrites, people who enjoyed polished speeches and the striking of attitudes but who, above all, wanted to lead an undisturbed life. Again and again he came across those who 'did not want to cause any trouble', who felt that they should submit to the authorities of the country 'which had so generously provided asylum' and whose own passivity led them to spread insinuations against activists such as Sabate, who were incapable of remaining inactive in the face of tyranny. It was precisely because he was not an elitist that when he found the Committees had failed him he travelled around desperately from one comrade to another, hoping that someone would come up with a scheme for the struggle against Franco in which he could be of some use. His eternal question was, 'Have you got anything going in regard to Spain? Can I help you in any way?' The dream of Sabate's life was to stop being a *'franctireur'* and to take part in organized activity which would lead to the downfall of General Franco. Meetings bored him to tears – he wanted to get on with planning projects. He could not understand suggestions that the time was not opportune, when beyond the Pyrenees people were suffering under the dictatorship. *El Quico* met comrades who, like himself had similar ideas and the same feeling of despair and importance when they saw the manner in which the libertarian Organization behaved in exile. So it was that once again, without the support of the Organization, Sabate prepared a new stage of activities in Spain with the meagre means he had at his disposal. He managed to bring together a small group of comrades. Together they constructed and designed some strange new weapons. He experimented with these activities in the countryside around Dijon with reasonably satisfactory results, and it was only due to bad luck that he was prevented from using them against the tyranny in Spain.

While in prison he had been seriously ill with a stomach complaint, and in the autumn of 1958 his health deteriorated rapidly. He was rushed to the Regional Hospital in Dijon where, on 3 November, he was operated on for a serious gastric ulcer. On three previous occasions he had been obliged to attend hospital with this complaint but always, at the last moment, he had left without undergoing surgery, hoping vainly that an effective treatment might be discovered in the near future. On this occasion, however, he allowed the operation to be performed when he found he had no option.

The reason Francisco feared the operating table was, above all, because of the necessity of anaesthetics – he dreaded being unconscious in the hands of people he did not know and who could do what they pleased with his life while he was incapable of defending himself. Although not obsessive, he suspected that Franco's agents would one day try to assassinate him. His immobilization during the operation would give them the perfect opportunity. Prior to the operation *El Quico* pleaded with his friends to promise that while he was unconscious they would not leave him unattended for one moment. As his friends could not take much time off work they decided to contact Sabate's wife, Leonor, still in Toulouse, thinking she would be the best person to look after him. She arrived in Dijon just before the operation took place. There, at Sabate's bedside, she explained to him that after his friends had called her she had gone to the Organization's Headquarters in the Rue Belfort in Toulouse, where they had given her 50,000 francs to cover her expenses.

He reacted violently to this information. Struggling into a sitting position he took from beneath his pillow a bundle containing 60,00 francs which his employer had given him that same day as wages due, and handed them to Leonor. 'Take this,' he said. 'When you get back to Toulouse give them back their money untouched. I want nothing to do with them!'

The operation was a success and Leonor spent the next twenty-four hours by his bedside, without moving once. His friends also spent all their free time with him. After a fortnight the hospital told him he was being discharged and as he had no family registered in Dijon he was being sent for convalescence to an old people's home. His friends bridled at the suggestion, which they felt was an insult, and he went to stay at the house of one of the local comrades. Two or three days later the wound began to suppurate, but Sabate absolutely refused to return to the hospital. Instead his friend's wife nursed him back to health. With *El Quico*'s robust constitution it did not take long for him to recover completely, putting on nearly nine pounds in ten days – though he had lost much more. Once again his high spirits and optimism returned.

About the middle of December he thanked his friends gratefully for the loving care and attention they had given him, but as he now felt perfectly fit and well he preferred to go his own way. He had already spent too much time inactive. He wanted once more to take up the struggle against Franco, and needed to be on his own. In this way he would not compromise anyone as a result of his activities. He moved into a rented flat at No. 2 Fontaine-Saint-Anne, and began visiting comrades in Paris and other French cities.

Shortly after moving into the flat he received a letter from Angel M.U., who was serving thirty years in a Spanish prison, and who had caused him so many problems. The repression in Spain following the *Cubiertas y Tejados* affair sprang directly from Angel's arrest. However, Sabate had looked after his defence and had sent money to him regularly while he was in prison. In the letter Angel complained that while he was rotting

189

in a Spanish dungeon Sabate was 'living like a lord' in France. Sabate shook his head sadly at this unjust accusation, and said to his friends, 'You see how I cannot give up the struggle.'

A little later he made the final preparations for his group to return to Spain. Before leaving he wanted to spend a few days with his daughters in Toulouse and so, on 28 December, 1958, petitioned the Ministry of the Interior, through the Prefect of the Department of the Côte d'Or, with a medical certificate stating that he should spend sometime convalescing with his family. His hopes were dashed, however, when the Prefect received the following ministerial reply:

> I beg to inform you that I consider it to be totally out of the question that this foreigner should be allowed to return to the Department of the Haute Garonne, and with good reason, since his access to this area is forbidden by a pro-hibition of residence order made against him dated 8 April, 1958, in accordance with the decision of Montpellier Court of Appeal (18-12-1957) which sentenced him to six months imprisonment and five years restricted residence.
>
> I would be grateful if you would inform the person concerned of this decision etc.

His friends advised him not to make any final decision concerning his proposed journey to Spain until the Tenth Congress of Inter-Continental Groups of the MLE/CNT, fixed for August 1959 in Toulouse, had taken place. This meeting was cancelled on the orders of the Prefecture of Police, but it was held later in Vierzon in the Department of Cher, from 9 to 13 September. Hoping that some positive line would result from this conference, Sabate attended all the preliminary local meetings and was made a delegate to the full regional meeting. Together with many other militants he shared the illusion that this congress would at last bring about confederal unity, which he firmly supported, and that the libertarian movement in exile

190

might once again become an effective force.[8] At the Congress in Vierzon he had only observer's status, but he followed the discussions with avid interest. He went round speaking to everyone who appeared to him more or less to have the same ideas and propositions. The answers he got were all the same, wait . . . wait . . . wait. He remained until the end of the conference and still the same old result – the lion had spawned the usual mouse. 'Another year lost,' he said grimly.

Everywhere he was confronted with the same apathy. However, the fact of the matter was that this time Sabate could no longer wait – even if he wanted to. The spectre of the Rhône Poulenc case returned to haunt him. After twice having brought up the case and twice being forced to bring a stay to suspend the hearing, the Prosecutor now wanted to bring him up for trial again. Repeated petitions by his lawyers were rejected out of hand and, finally, on 5 November, 1959 the Lyons Procurator arraigned Sabate before the Appeal Court. The hearing took place on 7 December and its decision was as follows :

> Under Article 617 of the Code of Criminal Proceedings this registered letter is to inform Francisco Sabate Llopart, accused of attempted robbery with violence and wilful murder, domiciled in Dijon (Côte d'Or) 2, Rue de la Fontaine, Ste-Anne, in the house of M. Petit, that in the Criminal Court on 5 November, 1959, the Court has rejected his request that proceedings should not be made against him in accordance with the deposition made on 20 February, 1959 before the Appeal Court of Lyons.

THE PROCURATOR GENERAL

Sabate was by now sick and tired of the whole judicial mess. He had not the slightest intention of going back to a French prison and was advised by many of his friends to emigrate to

South America.

'Since when has South America been next to Spain?' he asked.

His period of waiting had come to an end. He began equipping his expedition to Spain and gathered around him the enthusiastic friends who were to accompany him. Behind he left many other comrades who were prepared to come to his signal once he established his first bases.

However, this time Sabate underestimated the growing efficiency of the Spanish Special Branch and International Police co-operation across the frontiers. At that very moment the ex-Chief of the Special Services Brigade, Pedro Polo Borreguero, who specialized in the persecution of the anarcho-syndicalists – was in France, ostensibly as an attaché to the Spanish Embassy in Paris. *El Quico* was warned of the dangers he was running, but what could he do? During his trips and at meetings he took every precaution. Even when he returned to Dijon he always had someone waiting for him at the station with a platform ticket so that it could not be proved that he had actually left the city. This time none of the precautions he took were sufficient – this time the odds against him were too great. Weighed down as he was by the measures of confinement imposed upon him, Franco's agents watched his every move, spying upon him directly or from information from the French police.

On his way back to Spain on 1 December, 1959, Sabate telephoned a friend in Paris. 'My regards to everyone. Thanks for everything until the next time we meet . . . if there is a next time!'

At the end of December a comrade in Dijon received a card post-marked Narbonne, written in an unknown hand and signature, saying that due to the bad weather Sabate was suspending his journey into Spain until the spring. The origin of this card remains a mystery. On 5 January, 1960 radio and television news flashes announced the death of Sabate and the four comrades who had accompanied him.

El Quico had crossed the frontier near Coustouges at the end of December. Accompanying him were twenty-nine-year-old Antonio Miracle Guitart; twenty-seven-year-old Rogelio Madrigal Torres; thirty-nine-year-old Francisco Conesa Alvarez; and twenty-year-old Martin Ruiz Montoya.[9] The Spanish Security Service knew of Sabate's impending arrival from the French police, and the Guardia Civil had prepared a reception at the frontier worthy of Sabate and his reputation. They had set up posts, patrols and surveillance units in all the mountains of the area. They were watching and guarding cross-roads and main roads, as well as the approaches to the towns and villages. All cottages in isolated areas were watched day and night by units of three Guardia. This time they were prepared for all eventualities and reinforcements had been billeted in the neighbouring towns of Besalu, Beuda and Albana. Also farmers, charcoal-burners and wood-cutters had all been warned that they must inform the troops immediately of the presence of any strangers in their area.

From the many statements, depositions and accounts of the final episode in Sabate's life we have tried to reconstruct as far as possible the movements of Francisco and his group until the final tragedy a few days later.

A Guardia Civil post at Llado reported sighting five men dressed in blue overalls, mountain boots and rucksacks in the area of the River Manol at four-thirty in the afternoon. A couple of hours later, two men, dressed in blue overalls, presented themselves at a nearby farmhouse, passing themselves off as smugglers and buying a quantity of food. A short time later these same men were seen in the company of another three going in the direction of the River Muga, as though they were heading for the French frontier. This information was collated and sent to the Guardia Civil Commander, who ordered immediate strengthening of all patrols in the vicinity. The following day, 31 December, a mountain patrol of Guardia Civil, after unsuccessfully questioning small farmers and charcoal-burners in the valley of Maya de Moncalt, took up a position on the mountain slope which commanded a view of the whole valley. About eight o'clock that morning they noticed smoke coming out of the *Casot y Falgos* farmhouse, which they knew to be deserted. One of the Guardia rode over to investigate and was met by a hail of machine-gun fire. He let himself fall as if dead and saw five men run for the cover of the mountainside. Now there was no doubt : it was Sabate and his group. The ground was heavily overgrown with trees and bushes so the comrades managed to shake off their pursuers without any great difficulty, but they could have had no idea of the enormous number of troops deployed in the area to prevent them reaching Barcelona alive.

The Guardia returned to the nearby village of Maya and telephoned to headquarters in Besalu, and within a short time every available unit was despatched to the scene of the gun-fight. But the comrades had managed to cover their tracks and disappear. The next reported sighting of the group was at noon that same day, when they were seen heading in the direction of the village of Espinavesa to the south-east. This time they were reported to be progressing warily, with their arms at the ready. The man in charge of the operation was a colonel commanding the 24th Battalion of the Guardia Civil, and he decided to try to encircle the area in which the group were last sighted – Borrasa, Tarabaus, Llado, Crespia and all bridges and possible crossing points along the Fluvia River.

The last information as to the whereabouts of the group on the 31st indicated that they were still heading in a southerly direction and were within a few miles of the Fluvia River. About ten o'clock that night patrols in the vicinity of the village of La Palma reported hearing the cries of quails. Later it was discovered that the comrades carried quail whistles so it is likely that, in spite of the heavy guard, the group managed to cross the river during the night of 31 December.

The next day, 1 January, both banks of the river were thoroughly searched without finding any indication as to the whereabouts of Sabate and his group, so reinforcements were sent in the direction of Gerona, where it was thought they might be heading. It should be pointed out here that the Guardia Civil themselves were constantly being sent on wild goose chases by local peasants and labourers, so adding to the difficulties they were already facing.

On Sunday, 3 January, the group was located for the last time. The Guardia, keeping watch on a hilltop known as Castillo de la Mota, near Gerona, spotted them through binoculars entering the *Clara* farmhouse between Bañolas and Gerona. This was an unusually large number of people for a Sunday morning in a farmhouse occupied by an elderly married couple, Juan Salas and his wife Balbina Alonso. The Guardia suspected they were on to their quarry. An hour later the farmhouse, on the side of a wooded hill, was completely surrounded by troops. The area in front of the farm was clear, making it difficult for anyone to enter or leave without being noticed. As the Guardia approached cautiously, they saw three men come outside the front door and talk among themselves. The captain ordered his men to open fire on the group, killing one, Francisco Conesa Alvarez, immediately, and wounding another, Sabate, in the leg and buttock. *El Quico* and the other comrade managed to get back inside the house safely. The woman of the house tried to close the window shutters on hearing the sound of gunfire and was hit by a bullet in the hand. There was to be no quarter in this final battle. The siege was on.

To save ammunition, the besieged men used a shotgun they found in the house to head off the attack and, faced with this show of resistance, the besiegers decided to wait until nightfall before making any move to attack the house. One Guardia Civil, Jesus Gonzalez Otero, had already been wounded in the leg as he attempted to close in on the farm. His comrades also decided to wait until nightfall before bringing him in, and he remained there in agony for the rest of the day.

At five-thirty in the afternoon the commanding officer of the battalion, Lt-Col Rodrigo Gayet Girbal, arrived to take charge of the operation, and at ten-thirty ordered the distribution of fresh ammunition, hand-grenades, food and 'plenty of alcohol', as the report says, to 'heighten the morale of the troops'.

The battle continued during the remaining hours of daylight. The four comrades inside the farm waited impatiently for the disappearance of the moon to make their escape under cover of darkness. At one in the morning heavy clouds covered the sky and the night was plunged into darkness. It was a stroke of luck, they felt – the perfect moment. During the day *El Quico* had prepared an escape route by knocking a hole in the floor which led to the stables adjoining the back of the house – avoiding the front which was commanded by the guns of the Guardia Civil. Under cover of darkness they hustled a cow through the door of the stable and immediately the besiegers opened fire on the moving object. Having diverted the fire of the Guardia, two of the group ran off in the opposite direction into the woods, but the guns of the Guardia Civil were waiting for them there too. With no place to hide, they were both shot down in a hail of sudden death.

Sabate also tried to escape, but instead of running as his two comrades had done, he threw himself on the ground and crawled along quickly to the cover of some nearby scrub – only to discover that the Guardia Civil were thinking along the same lines and were within a few yards of him. Lying there, flat, motionless, scarcely daring to breathe, he heard someone crawling towards him from the opposite direction saying, 'Don't shoot . . . I'm the Lieutenant.' It was this Lieutenant of the Guardia Civil, Francisco Fuentes, who was fated to meet *El Quico* face to face, though he was never to know it. Sabate shot him in the head at point-blank range, killing him immediately. The other besiegers could not tell where and from whom the shot had come so Sabate, reacting immediately, began to crawl in the direction in which the lieutenant had just come, repeating his words, 'Don't shoot . . . I'm the Lieutenant.' In this way he managed to crawl through three lines of Guardia Civil.

At dawn the following day, 4 January, the troops found the body of the officer and Sabate's three comrades, but two were still missing. They fired a few shots at the house to see if it was still occupied, but when there was no reply, two of their number went in under covering fire. They got into the house without difficulty and found the married couple lying terrified in one of the back rooms, and proceeded to search all the rooms and outhouses. The bake-house was under the main building, and the Guardia, suspecting that someone was hiding in there, and being unwilling to run any further risks threw a couple of tear-gas bombs inside. From the boiler itself there stumbled a blind and half-suffocated figure who was cut to ribbons by the deadly hail of lead as he ran through the doorway. This was the fourth of the group, Martin Ruiz, but search as they may they could not find the fifth. They could hardly credit it, but in the end they had to admit that *El Quico* had escaped, slipping through the hands of over a hundred highly-trained and well-armed men!

When they reported their failure to Barcelona the orders came back sharply : Find him without losing a second!

Such was the excitement at the prospect of catching their quarry that even Eduardo Quintela, the ex-Chief Commissioner of the Brigada Politico Social in Barcelona, now living in retirement in Galicia and a long standing enemy of the Libertarian Movement, came rushing to the scene when he heard that his old adversary was besieged in Sarria de Ter, bringing with him his faithful companion – a bloodhound. He wanted to take part personally in the hunt for Sabate. Quintela could not miss being in at the kill of the man who had caused him so much humiliation and ridicule in the course of his career.

However, the huntsmen and their dogs soon lost the trail. Sabate had learned during many years in the mountains to include in his equipment a packet of pepper to confuse his scent.

Although he had a few hours advantage over his pursuers, his situation was critical. They would know, from the farmer and his wife, that he was badly wounded. During the battle he had been hit in the neck, buttock and leg by the Guardia Civil's bullets. He was in considerable pain and only by drawing on all his reserves was he able to continue his flight. Before daybreak on 5 January, *El Quico* managed to reach the Fornells de la Selva railway station, after swimming the River Ter, some twelve miles to the south of Gerona. It was incredible that he had managed to travel so far in his condition. At six-thirty that morning a mail train left Gerona, coming from Port Bou, which stopped at every station as far as Massanet. Sabate remained hidden at the end of the railway platform until the train started, and then jumped into the cab, pistol in hand. The engine driver, Pedro Garcia Marcos, and the fireman, Joaquin Puig, looked at the man as though he were mad. He calmed their fears and asked for something to eat, as he was starving. They gave him their sandwiches, which he ate voraciously and then told them to carry on their normal procedure.

'Get the train going. Don't stop until you get to Barcelona!'

They were staggered. 'To Barcelona?' The driver explained to *El Quico* that this was impossible as they had to exchange the steam engine they were driving for an electric one in Massanet. Besides, they had to obey the signals along the line. Sabate did not insist. Perhaps in his heart he had not expected they could really carry out his wish to get to Barcelona, *his* Barcelona, as soon as possible.

In Massanet, the train stopped to change engines and, when it was ready to leave for Barcelona, the steam engine reversed onto another line. As it passed Sabate jumped from one to the other, bidding farewell to one crew and introducing himself to another in one breath. He left the crew of the first train in Massanet to recount their extraordinary adventure. He had no doubts about the result. Before leaving them he had asked that they should not mention his presence but in spite of this, fully expected a gala reception at the next station.

The train reached Fornells de la Selva at eight in the morning. Sabate, who was watching the track, ordered the driver to reduce speed as the train went round the bend only a few thousand yards from the station. The driver obeyed and in seconds sped off without his passenger.

From Fornells de la Selva *El Quico* managed to travel another forty-five miles towards Barcelona, but the city of his dreams was still very far away. By now he could scarcely walk, as his leg was badly infected and his mind clouded with fever. Nevertheless, he told himself he had managed to drag himself as far as the slopes of the Sierra de Montseny – only a few miles more and he would be able to rest himself in its magnificent forest, among its oaks and chestnuts, its beeches and cork trees, its maples and yews, which he had often wandered among as a young boy. He knew its paths and its tracks, every corner of its green woodlands – there he could escape an army and would be safe. This salvation so near, was too far for him. He was weakening rapidly and would die if he did not get medical attention soon.

San Celoni was in sight. Gasping, exhausted, he struggled towards it. A peasant was busy by the roadside fixing his cart and Sabate hailed him, asking for something to drink to soothe his burning fever. The man readily gave him a flask of wine which Sabate drained in one gulp. The man was going into the village and offered *El Quico* a lift. In San Celoni, when the man had left him, Sabate asked an old woman who appeared reliable for a doctor. It turned out there was only one in the village, but she gave him the address – in the Calle de Jose Antonio. She added that at this time of day it was doubtful whether he would find the doctor at home. In that event he was told to go to the doctor's driver, who lived just opposite the doctor's house and who would be able to tell him where the doctor was and at what time he would return.

As the old lady had said, the doctor was not at home. *El Quico* then stumbled across the road to knock on the door of the house opposite, No. 26, but in his fever he mistook the number. A man by the name of Francisco Berrenguer Roca lived there. When Berrenguer opened the door and saw the stranger in such a terrible condition asking for the doctor's chauffeur he replied rudely that it was the wrong house.

El Quico, more dead than alive, said, 'It doesn't matter to me! Let me in to lie down for a bit, please.'

Berrengeur said no, and roughly pushed the wounded stranger from his doorway. As he did so he felt the sub-machine-gun Sabate had hidden under his coat. Panicking,

Berrenguer instinctively seized the gun and would not let go. The two men, pushing and shouting, wrestled each other out into the street towards the corner of the Calle Jose Antonio and Santa Tecla.

In the meantime the news that Sabate might have arrived in San Celoni had reached the Guardia Civil, and they, in turn, called out the local Militia[10] to go to the station as reinforcements. At the station they found that Sabate, or at least a man answering his description, had gone in the direction of the village, so the Militia patrols were therefore sent to search all the streets of San Celoni.

In one of the patrols there was a Militia corporal (who was also local Secretary of the Falangist National Syndicalist Central [CNS]) named Abel Rocha Sanz, and another Militia man, Jose Sibina Morull, accompanying a sergeant of the Guardia Civil by the name of Martinez Collado. This patrol was passing near the Calle Jose Antonio, when they heard the cries for help of the man with whom Sabate was desperately struggling for his life. The patrol split up, Rocha taking one side of the street, the sergeant and Sibina going round the block so that they could get Sabate in a cross-fire.

In his fight to get away from Berrenguer, Sabate, with what little energy that remained, bit his assailant hard on the hand – almost removing one of Berrenguer's fingers. Abel Rocha fired his first bullet, which missed Sabate and hit Berrenguer wounding him badly. This enabled Sabate to wrench himself free and fire with his Colt. He was exhausted and, panting for breath, did not have time to mount the Thompson gun still under his coat – nevertheless, his pistol was sufficient to hit the Militia man in the right leg near the knee-cap. The wounded Rocha, however, was still able to fire with his automatic rifle, and his bullet hit Sabate at the same moment as another from the Guardia Civil sergeant behind. The fight was over. Sabate lay dead. The Militia man riddled his corpse with bullets as it lay on the pavement, just in case.

And so, at eight-thirty in the morning of 5 January, 1960 the eventful life of Francisco Sabate Llopart came to an end. He died as one thinks he would have wanted to die and to no one better could one apply these words of Thucydides':

> For a manly spirit more bitter is humiliation associated with cowardice than death when it comes unperceived in close company with stalwart deeds and public hopes.

To die cut down in battle was the only death worthy of a man who had refused to adapt himself to the corruption of an age and to surrender to the conqueror. A man who risked everything in an attempt to tear out that bloody chapter, written by Franco, in the history of Spain.

Sabate was buried in the old San Celoni cemetery in an unconsecrated grave. The doctor who carried out the autopsy revealed that the glory in which those who thought they had taken Sabate's life were revelling, was premature. The bullets of the Militia man and the Guardia Civil had killed a man who was already dead. The wound in his leg was gangrenous and even if, on reaching San Celoni, he had been taken straight to hospital and treated with all that modern science had to offer, it would still have been too late. He was beyond saving.

Radio Luxembourg gave the tragic news of his death to the world at one-thirty pm on 5 January. When the news of his death reached Barcelona, the people refused to believe that it was true. They dismissed it as a police machination. For the people some men are immortal. The Catalan workers said, and kept on saying, 'You'll see, *El Quico* will soon be back.'

Francisco Sabate, *El Quico*, will never return to Barcelona. He will never see the new Spain that will rise to honour him as a symbol of those who struggled, in a battle not yet ended, for the emancipation of man.

[1] Born 12 April, 1916, he joined the force in July 1941 as a policeman 'second class', but due to his zeal rapidly gained promotion and is now Principal Commissar of the Barcelona Brigada Politico Social.

[2] Born 27 March, 1916, joined the force in July 1934. He acted as Secretary during the interrogation.

[3] The VIIth Full International Conference of the FAI took place in July 1956, to coincide with the VIIth Inter-Continental Congress of the MLE-CNT in Toulouse. Maria attended the FAI meeting where the activities of the *Grupos Anarco-Sindicalistas* were discussed, but she was hardly allowed to open her mouth to protest. The meeting approved the following resolution: 'The position of the *Grupos Anarco-Sindicalistas* in exile is to be condemned!'

[4] Sabate sent the Organization three letters dated 15 August, 1 September and 8 September, 1957. We only give the third one here, which summarizes his activities and ideas.

[5] One of the lawyers who acted on instructions from Sabate was Jean-Baptiste Biaggi, a well-known French advocate.

[6] Considered an expert of social repression, he was made Secretary-General of Security in, September 1951, succeeding Lt Col Alfonso Romero de Arcos, who had held the post since September 1949.

[7] Facerias was born in Barcelona on 6 January, 1920. During the Spanish Civil War he fought in the Ascaso Column and was taken prisoner during the last battles in Catalonia. Freed in 1945, he dedicated himself to clandestine revolutionary activity and was, among other things, Defence Secretary of the Catalan Young Libertarians.

[8] The unity of the *Movimiento Libertario Espanol* (MLE) was finally decided at the first International Congress of the Spanish CNT in exile, in Limoges in August 1960. Three months later, in November 1960, under the chairmanship of the veteran militant Cipriano Mera, the reuniting of the Libertarian Trade Union Movement was announced publicly at a meeting in the Alhambra Theatre in Paris.

[9] Miracle was born on 20 November, 1930 in Brafin (Tarragona) and lived in Clermont Ferrand where he worked as a builder's labourer.

Torres was born on 5 November, 1933 in Hospitalet de Llobregat (Barcelona) and lived in Dijon where he worked as a bricklayer. He had deserted from the Spanish Army and went to France in 1956.

Alvarez was born in Barcelona on 21 December, 1921, and went to France in 1950 where he worked as a driver.

Montoya was born in Provins (Seine & Marne) on 13 April, 1939. He was French born of Spanish parents and lived in Lyons.

[10] This Militia (*Somaten*) was an armed civilian militia peculiar to Catalonia. It was reorganized during the dictatorship of General Primo de Rivera (1923-30) by General Severiano Martinez Anido, as a reserve force in times of unrest.

Epilogue

For some days after his death, a great deal of space was devoted in the international press to Francisco Sabate. Seldom had the death of an Anarchist received such wide coverage. Why were they so interested? Perhaps it was the spectacular nature of his escape from the cordon of the Guardia Civil. But his four comrades – Miracle, Madrigal, Conesa and Martin Ruiz – died in anonymity.

At first the world's newspapers carried the headline with the fascist trademark – 'Death of a Bandit' – later they came to understand that the word 'bandit' did not exactly fit Sabate, and they began to vary their approach, while introducing new errors. For instance, there were idiotic suggestions that Sabate had returned to Spain merely to avenge the murder of his brothers.

The Libertarian Movement in exile had the opportunity and the means to correct the lies and errors of the press. But the Organization preferred to bury its head in the sand. The most unpardonable barbarities came from self-professed libertarians. For instance, the weekly paper *CNT* printed an article by its then editor, Jose Peirats, on 17 January, 1960:

> I do not wish to judge Sabate or to think of harshly as do those who have complained many times of the fact that his activity has caused injury to the CNT, against whose decisions he rebelled, and even – something which should never come from one who has taken part in it – endeavoured

to supplant. Neither do I want to make a hero of him, another Empecinado, another Durruti. Nor should the courts of Spain or elsewhere presume to pass judgement on someone when they themselves have passed beyond all norms of ordinary life and conduct.

I do not want to see in his obsession, in his unreasoning and unreasonable determination to go into Spain against any possible individual or collective interest, anything other than something which can completely absolve him in many eyes, or certainly in my own: the despair of his soul, the determination *to avenge his murdered brothers*, the ideal that he had converted into so great an obsession that it made every other consideration a secondary one. [*Author's italics*] One could put down the libels of the capitalist press to ignorance. This statement could not be so excused.

The death of his brothers did affect Sabate deeply, but the pain he felt did not supply the motives for his struggle. He did not seek vengeance, something which never entered his head, but social justice. To say otherwise not only deliberately slanders the man, but is deliberately deceitful when it comes from those who knew him. Francisco Sabate – as we have tried to show in these pages – gave himself to the struggle long before his brothers died. He continued as he began – with the hope of an insurrection by the Spanish people and the consequent destruction of the Franco régime.

In another paper of the Organization *Solidaridad Obrera* (Paris edition, 21 January, 1960) one piece managed to reach the pinnacle of hypocrisy. It carried a photograph of Sabate, but no article or any reference to his struggle. Instead, it confined itself to refuting a sentence which the international press had claimed were Sabate's last words – '*Viva la muerte*'.[1]

The article concluded the gross insult to Sabate's memory with the pious truism: 'The Anarchist fights for everyone's life and in extreme cases, loses his own. But he never commits the solecism of shouting "Long live death!" like any totalitarian general.'

The height of impudence, however, was reached in an article carried by the anarcho-syndicalist paper *CNT* published on 7 February, 1960. The article was signed by a friend of Miracle, one of the young men who died with Sabate, and read :

> There are still many young men, many unknown people, who could also be cannon fodder – young men who, precisely because of their youth and idealism, are easily manipulated in the hands of evil men.

There was one reasonably satisfying and objective report, heard on the Spanish service of Belgrade Radio in a broadcast on 14 January, 1960 :

> Dear listeners : Our correspondent Rade Nikolic will give a short talk on Francisco Sabate, the Catalan revolutionary murdered last week by the Francoist police . . .
>
> Francisco Sabate, known as *El Quico*, militant of the CNT and one of the most outstanding defenders of the republican and democratic cause of the Spanish people . . .
>
> This is not the proper time to discuss the different methods of struggle, nor to applaud or condemn this or that form of revolutionary action. What is important is that the enemies of the people should not be allowed to stain the memory of a revolutionary who, in his own words, felt ashamed to be alive when his brothers and most of his comrades had been murdered . . .

The broadcast ended with these words : 'You have just heard our reporter Rade Nikolic give a talk on the life of the Catalan revolutionary Francisco Sabate.'

A few days later a Zagreb daily newspaper, *Vjesnik u*

Sridjedu (20 January, 1960) published an illustrated article on Sabate entitled '*El Quico*, fought for twenty-four years. The death of a legendary combatant against the Franco tyranny.'

Soon, too, the more scrupulous newspapers of the bourgeois press began to look at Sabate with more respect. Behind the lies and distortions they began to perceive the silhouette of a guerrilla and view with sympathy the real Sabate, the man of the libertarian resistance, 'Public Enemy No. 1' of Franco's Fascist State.

But perhaps the best epitaph was written eight years before Sabate's death. This is what Felipe Alaiz de Pablo[2] wrote in issue number 368 of *Solidaridad Obrera*, published in Paris, 15 March, 1952:

> Rightly or wrongly, anxious or not for fame and historical renown, perhaps more sentimentally than coolly inclined towards an absolute nihilism, probably scornful of the gregarious and passive mass for whom they sacrifice themselves without expecting help from it, more attached sometimes to anonymity than to an accumulation of redentorist reverence – for religions are founded upon the spectacular sacrifice of one, and only one, in favour of the comfort and passivity of the rest – the activists, facing danger, dedicate their lives to their cause, and with their own lives pay.
>
> The persistent ones finish in the hands of the terrorist State, while the terrorist but passive *ideologues* and terror-inspired masses keep away from danger while applauding these isolated fighters, but never ready themselves, these shy inhibited ones, to take direct part in the struggle.

Slowly, the Organization in Paris took the decision to vindicate Sabate publicly – although always with a certain discretion. A document issued by it stated that 'Francisco Sabate Llopart was never, as stated by sections of the press and radio, a "bandit". He was a militant of the Anarcho-Syndicalist Action Groups and was killed by the fascist forces of General Franco because of his struggle for the freedom of Spain.'

In Paris too, not elsewhere, they began a collection for the families of *El Quico* and his four comrades. But at no point did they wish to concede the same honours to Jose Lluis Facerias, who had fallen in the same struggle, but perhaps in less spectacular circumstances, or even to Goliardo Fiaschi, at present in the Italian prison of Lecce, fifteen years later, handed over from a Spanish jail to an Italian one, a living symbol of the victims of the unity between Franco's Spain and Fascist Italy.

But the sincerest tribute to Sabate was the fact that his enemies in Spain celebrated his defeat with medals and honours for the police service. The press carried full reports supplied to it by Police Headquarters and the Directorate of Security. One and all referred to their fallen enemy as the *terrible bandit* Francisco Sabate Llopart.

---

[1] 'Long live death' was in fact the favourite slogan of General Millan de Astray, the badly scarred, mutilated, one-eyed, one-armed war veteran of the Spanish Army, one of the most blood-thirsty generals of the Franco régime. For Sabate to have used a phrase associated with such a reactionary figure would have been highly unlikely, and the suggestion that he did a gross libel upon him. Some foreign journalists, knowing the phrase as 'Spanish' but having forgotten or never having known General Millan de Astray, may have attributed it to Sabate to give 'colour' to their story. Perhaps he said, as many did, *'Viva la Anarquia!'*

[2] Felipe Alaiz, Anarchist writer and journalist, was born in Alarbate de Linca (Huesca). He died in Paris at the age of seventy-two on 8 April, 1959.